1st EDITION

Perspectives on Diseases and Disorders

Dissociative Disorders

Sylvia Engdahl
Book Editor

GALE
CENGAGE Learning

Detroit • New York • San Francisco • New Haven, Conn • Waterville, Maine • London

Elizabeth Des Chenes, *Director, Publishing Solutions*

© 2013 Greenhaven Press, a part of Gale, Cengage Learning

Gale and Greenhaven Press are registered trademarks used herein under license.

For more information, contact:
Greenhaven Press
27500 Drake Rd.
Farmington Hills, MI 48331-3535
Or you can visit our Internet site at gale.cengage.com

For product information and technology assistance, contact us at

Gale Customer Support, 1-800-877-4253
For permission to use material from this text or product, submit all requests online at
www.cengage.com/permissions

Further permissions questions can be e-mailed to permissionrequest@cengage.com

Articles in Greenhaven Press anthologies are often edited for length to meet page requirements. In addition, original titles of these works are changed to clearly present the main thesis and to explicitly indicate the author's opinion. Every effort is made to ensure that Greenhaven Press accurately reflects the original intent of the authors. Every effort has been made to trace the owners of copyrighted material.

Cover image © Ibex Anubis/Alamy

LIBRARY OF CONGRESS CATALOGING-IN-PUBLICATION DATA

Dissociative disorders / Sylvia Engdahl, book editor.
   p. cm. -- (Perspectives on diseases and disorders)
  Includes bibliographical references and index.
  ISBN 978-0-7377-6353-9 (hardcover)
  1. Dissociative disorders. 2. Dissociation (Psychology) I. Engdahl, Sylvia.
  RC553.D5D557 2012
  616.85'23--dc23

                                                                2012023735

Printed in the United States of America
1 2 3 4 5 6 7 16 15 14 13 12

CONTENTS

CHAPTER 2   Controversies Concerning
Dissociative Disorders

FOREWORD

"Medicine, to produce health, has to examine disease."
—Plutarch

Independent research on a health issue is often the first step to complement discussions with a physician. But locating accurate, well-organized, understandable medical information can be a challenge. A simple Internet search on terms such as "cancer" or "diabetes," for example, returns an intimidating number of results. Sifting through the results can be daunting, particularly when some of the information is inconsistent or even contradictory. The Greenhaven Press series Perspectives on Diseases and Disorders offers a solution to the often overwhelming nature of researching diseases and disorders.

From the clinical to the personal, titles in the Perspectives on Diseases and Disorders series provide students and other researchers with authoritative, accessible information in unique anthologies that include basic information about the disease or disorder, controversial aspects of diagnosis and treatment, and first-person accounts of those impacted by the disease. The result is a well-rounded combination of primary and secondary sources that, together, provide the reader with a better understanding of the disease or disorder.

Each volume in Perspectives on Diseases and Disorders explores a particular disease or disorder in detail. Material for each volume is carefully selected from a wide range of sources, including encyclopedias, journals, newspapers, nonfiction books, speeches, government documents, pamphlets, organization newsletters, and position papers. Articles in the first chapter provide an authoritative, up-to-date overview that covers symptoms, causes and effects, treatments, cures, and medical advances. The second chapter presents a substantial number of opposing viewpoints on controversial treatments and other current debates relating to the volume topic. The third chapter offers a variety of personal perspectives on the disease or disorder. Patients, doctors, caregivers, and loved ones represent just some of the voices found in this narrative chapter.

Each Perspectives on Diseases and Disorders volume also includes:

- An **annotated table of contents** that provides a brief summary of each article in the volume.
- An **introduction** specific to the volume topic.
- Full-color **charts and graphs** to illustrate key points, concepts, and theories.
- Full-color **photos** that show aspects of the disease or disorder and enhance textual material.
- **"Fast Facts"** that highlight pertinent additional statistics and surprising points.
- A **glossary** providing users with definitions of important terms.
- A **chronology** of important dates relating to the disease or disorder.
- An annotated list of **organizations to contact** for students and other readers seeking additional information.
- A **bibliography** of additional books and periodicals for further research.
- A detailed **subject index** that allows readers to quickly find the information they need.

Whether a student researching a disorder, a patient recently diagnosed with a disease, or an individual who simply wants to learn more about a particular disease or disorder, a reader who turns to Perspectives on Diseases and Disorders will find a wealth of information in each volume that offers not only basic information, but also vigorous debate from multiple perspectives.

INTRODUCTION

Dissociative disorders are the most controversial of the conditions seen by mental health professionals. Some psychiatrists do not think they exist as separate syndromes because dissociation is often a symptom of other disorders. Others accept the reality of some dissociative disorders but not all, and there is disagreement about their cause and treatment even among those who believe all the defined types are distinct conditions.

Dissociation is an altered state of consciousness in which a person feels detached from aspects of everyday experience. Exactly which mental phenomena the term covers varies, depending on different scientists' views; it has been studied for only a few decades and is not fully understood. Mild, brief dissociation is normal—for example, when someone is daydreaming or is deeply absorbed in a book, movie, or video game or has gone a long time without sleep. But when this state persists and interferes with a person's ongoing ability to function, it is deemed pathological, or abnormal. People who dissociate abnormally may perceive the world around them as dreamlike or unreal, or they may lose a sense of their identity, sometimes even of their own bodies. They may forget some or all of their personal history. Those with the most severe dissociation disorders develop a number of separate states of mind that seem like different personalities, each of which may be unaware of the others' existence.

When it occurs during extreme stress, dissociation is protective; it is a natural psychological mechanism that helps people to endure traumatic experiences they are unable to deal with. If it continues after the crisis is over, however, it becomes a problem. Dissociation disorders are believed to be caused by emotional trauma, and they indeed arise among people exposed to horrific violence, natural disaster, and war, but since the majority of people emerge from such traumas without developing a dissociation disorder—and there are also cases of people with such disorders who have never lived through a truly traumatic event—there appears to be something more involved. Scientists disagree on what or how much more.

The most common and least controversial dissociative disorder is depersonalization disorder, of which the main symptom is a feeling of detachment from self, sometimes as if watching from outside oneself or of being a robot. This often includes derealization, which means feeling one's surroundings are unreal. All emotions may be numbed, but on the other hand, people with depersonalization disorder may find it terrifying and think they are losing their sanity when actually they are not. They are likely to believe that no one else has ever had such feelings. Because many other mental disorders can produce dissociation or exist concurrently, sufferers from depersonalization disorder may not be correctly diagnosed and may not receive appropriate treatment for a long time, if ever. Learning that the condition is not rare makes it easier to accept.

A somewhat more serious dissociative disorder is dissociative amnesia, formerly called psychogenic or psychological amnesia to distinguish it from amnesia caused by brain injury. Amnesia is the inability to remember personal information such as what has happened in one's past life, or even one's identity. It may involve full loss of memory for specific periods and may last a short or a long time. There is a rare similar condition called dissociative fugue, now considered a separate disorder but soon to be listed as a subtype of dissociative amnesia, in which a person suddenly travels far from home and turns up in a strange city without knowing his or her name or origin.

All psychiatrists agree that these forms of dissociative amnesia occur. But there is another form that has aroused

Dissociation is an altered state of consciousness in which a person feels detached from aspects of everyday life, sometimes including one's own self. (© **LADA**/**Photo** **Researchers, Inc.**)

heated debate and has become one of the most contentious issues in America today, not only among therapists and patients but in the courts. Is it possible for an adult to have no memory whatsoever of being abused as a child and then all at once—either spontaneously or with the help of a therapist—recall terrible physical or sexual abuse? In the 1980s a great many cases of this kind appeared, and some therapists urged all women with unexplained emotional problems to attempt recovery of such memories, often under hypnosis. It was said that childhood sexual abuse must be more common than had been thought. Countless women remembered repeated incidents of it despite having previously believed their childhoods were happy. Many then accused their parents, suing them or even bringing criminal charges against them, and some parents who were innocent went to prison.

After a few years, with the clients of recovered memory therapists recalling more and more horrifying episodes not only of abuse within families but of participation in obscene satanic rituals, it became apparent that not all these accounts could be true. There were far too many of them; moreover, though child abuse does occur frequently, victims generally do not forget it. Yet people honestly believed they were regaining memories that had been repressed, and most of the therapists involved did not doubt that these memories were real. Then, in the 1990s, researchers found that false memories can indeed be produced by suggestion, often inadvertently, and that apart from external corroboration, there is no way to tell the difference between a true memory and a false one. To the human mind they feel just the same.

Today, the possibility of false memories is recognized although not yet understood, and some therapists have been sued for implanting them. Mental health professionals are warned to be careful not to ask leading questions that might facilitate the formation of false memories. Not all mental health professionals believe this can happen, however; some still insist that anyone who thinks he or she was abused really was, even if it was not recalled until much later. Some who purport these to be false memories, on the other hand, declare that dissociative amnesia with regard to child abuse cannot occur in someone who is otherwise normal. The American Psychological Association states that both phenomena exist, but many mental health experts continue to argue bitterly, displaying strong emotion and sometimes accusing each other of ulterior motives. The idea of memories being false makes people uncomfortable, for memory is an integral part of identity and they do not like to think that perhaps they cannot trust their own.

A still greater psychiatric controversy exists over the most serious dissociative order, dissociative identity disorder (DID), previously known as multiple personality disorder (MPD). People with DID have two or more alternating personality states, only one of which dominates consciousness at any given moment. When in one of these personality states—called alters—the person is often unaware of the existence of the others and has puzzling memory gaps covering hours, days, or weeks. Activities and even friends are different during each of these states, so the person may lack knowledge of things done when in another state, or if informed of them, may blame an alter. In different states he or she has different names, memories, and preferences, and may also show physical differences in such things as voice, visual acuity, handwriting, and occasionally medical conditions.

It is widely believed that the mind becomes compartmentalized in this way when a person, usually a child, tries to escape the pain of an intolerable situation, and, again, child abuse is generally blamed. However, some psychiatrists have pointed out that there is no evidence for this. Although many DID patients were abused as children, there are far more survivors of abuse who do not have DID, and although the condition is said to develop in childhood, few children display its symptoms. Moreover, child abuse has always existed, yet there were only a handful of DID cases before 1980. Since then, the condition has been estimated to affect from one out of a thousand people to one out of a hundred, and some say it is underdiagnosed. At first, patients with symptoms of DID had only two or three alters, but the average number kept increasing until there were people in whom therapy uncovered—or created—dozens or hundreds, some of which were perceived by the patient as not even human.

What caused the incredibly fast spread of DID? Many believe it was largely the result of sensational books, movies, and media reports that publicized the condition. Some maintain that the publicity led to discovery of authentic cases that would not otherwise have been detected. Others say it started a fad or created mass hysteria. Many psychiatrists believe that DID is not a real mental disorder but a manifestation of unconscious conformity to a socially created model or a therapist's interpretation of symptoms. At the opposite extreme are those who consider different alters so real that they treat them like separate people, as most of the patients do. Certainly DID patients dissociate in one abnormal way or another, and in most cases their suffering is real even if its origin is questionable.

There are exceptions, however. DID has occasionally been faked—because many courts accept the diagnosis at face value, criminals have sometimes been judged not guilty by reason of insanity on the grounds that one of their alters committed the crime, without the knowledge of the person on trial, when that was not true. Also, there is a growing number of people who perceive themselves as multiple and have the symptoms of DID, but do not view it as a disorder. They are able to function adequately despite having several separate personality states, and believe that as long as they are not harming anyone, they should not be called ill. They believe that they are given that label only because of society's prejudice against anyone who is different.

A resolution of the disagreements about dissociative amnesia and dissociative identity disorder does not appear to be in sight. Only further research and better scientific understanding of the nature of these conditions can bring it about.

In *Perspectives on Diseases and Disorders: Dissociative Disorders*, the contributors provide the latest science, discuss the current controversies, and convey the personal experiences associated with this challenging and frequently undiagnosed disease.

CHAPTER 1

Understanding Dissociative Disorders

An Overview of Dissociative Disorders

Rebecca J. Frey and Emily Jane Willingham

The authors of the following viewpoint explain that dissociative disorders are mental disorders in which a person's mind is detached from what is happening or compartmentalized so that he or she cannot consciously access all of it at once. Mild, brief dissociative experiences are normal, but when they persist or interfere with functioning, they are considered pathological. This can mean feeling unreal and separated from one's body, experiencing a loss of memory, or developing several separate identities. These reactions are usually preceded by trauma or extreme stress of some kind. There are four main types of dissociation disorders.

Rebecca J. Frey and Emily Jane Willingham are medical writers.

Photo on previous page. Dissociative disorders are often linked to post-traumatic stress such as past sexual or physical abuse.
(© Mira/Alamy)

The dissociative disorders are a group of mental disorders that affect consciousness and are defined as causing significant interference with the patient's general functioning, including social relationships and employment.

Dissociation is a mechanism that allows the mind to separate or compartmentalize certain memories or thoughts from normal consciousness. These split-off mental contents are not erased. They may resurface spontaneously or be triggered by objects or events in the person's environment.

Until recently, dissociation was widely considered to be a process that occurs along a spectrum of severity. It was considered a spectrum because people experiencing dissociation do not necessarily always have a dissociative disorder or other mental illness. A mild degree of dissociation occurs with some physical stressors; people who have gone without sleep for a long period of time, have had "laughing gas" for dental surgery, or have been in a minor accident often have brief dissociative experiences. As well, in another commonplace example of dissociation, people completely involved in a book or movie may not notice their surroundings or the passage of time. Yet another example might be driving on the highway and passing several exits without noticing or remembering. Dissociation is related to hypnosis in that hypnotic trance also involves a temporarily altered state of consciousness. Most patients with dissociative disorders are highly hypnotizable.

People in other cultures sometimes have dissociative experiences in the course of religious or other group activities (in certain trance states). These occurrences should not be judged in terms of what is considered "normal" in the United States.

Categories of Dissociation

Rather than the pathological forms of the disorder being considered a continuum, they now have been dichotomized into the categories of detachment and compartmentalization. Specific characteristics distinguish each of these, although there can be overlap. For example, compartmentalization might be characteristic of a form of dissociative disorder called dissociative amnesia. Patients who have the compartmentalized type of dissociation do not engage in conscious integration of mental systems and do not or cannot consciously access certain areas of memory or information that normally would be available. This type of dissociation also can occur in conversion disorder.

A person exhibiting the detachment form of a dissociation disorder experiences the altered state of consciousness that is more commonly associated with the concept of dissociation. In such cases, derealization or depersonalization are not merely transient, brief manifestations caused by lack of sleep. Instead, people with dissociation disorder may exhibit a flat affect (outward presentation of mood or emotion) and have a sense of being out of their own bodies. These detachment forms of dissociation may be associated with trauma and post-traumatic stress disorder, although post-traumatic stress disorder may also elicit crossover symptoms of compartmentalization. Recent studies of trauma indicate that the human brain stores traumatic memories in a different way than normal memories. Traumatic memories are not processed or integrated into a person's ongoing life in the same fashion as normal memories. Instead they are dissociated, or "split off," and may erupt into consciousness from time to time without warning. Affected people cannot control or "edit" these memories. Over a period of time, these two sets of memories, the normal and the traumatic, may coexist as parallel sets without being combined or blended. It has been suggested that the detachment may interfere with this process of consolidation. In extreme cases, different sets of dissociated memories may cause people to develop separate personalities for these memories—a disorder known as dissociative identity disorder (formerly called multiple personality disorder).

Studies suggest a frequency of pathological dissociation in the general North American population of between 2% and 3.3%. In Europe, reported rates are lower, at 0.3% in the nonclinical population and between 1.8% and 2.9% in student populations. Among psychiatric patients, frequency is much higher, between 5.4% and 12.7%, and it also is higher in groups with specific psychiatric diagnoses; for example, its frequency among women with eating disorders can be as high as 48.6%.

One type of dissociative disorder, dissociative amnesia, is characterized by a person's inability to remember certain events in his or her life. (© Carol and Mike Werner/Alamy)

Types of Dissociative Disorders

Dissociative amnesia is a disorder in which the distinctive feature is the patient's inability to remember important personal information to a degree that cannot be explained by normal forgetfulness. In many cases, it is a reaction to a traumatic accident or witnessing a violent crime. Patients with dissociative amnesia may develop depersonalization or trance states as part of the disorder, but they do not experience a change in identity.

Dissociative fugue is a disorder in which those affected temporarily lose their sense of personal identity and travel to other locations where they may assume a new identity. Again, this condition usually follows a major stressor or trauma. Apart from inability to recall their past or personal information, patients with dissociative fugue do not behave strangely or appear disturbed to others. Cases of dissociative fugue are more common in wartime or in communities disrupted by a natural disaster.

Depersonalization disorder is a disturbance in which the patient's primary symptom is a sense of detachment from the self. Depersonalization as a symptom (not as a disorder) is quite common in college-age populations. It is often associated with sleep deprivation or "recreational" drug use. It may be accompanied by "derealization" (where objects in an environment appear altered). Patients sometimes describe depersonalization as feeling like a robot or watching themselves from the outside.

Five Major Symptoms of Dissociative Disorders

- Amnesia—memory problems involving difficulty recalling personal information.

- Depersonalization—a sense of detachment or disconnection from one's self, or feeling like a stranger to one's self.

- Derealization—a sense of disconnection from familiar people or one's surroundings.

- Identity confusion or inner struggle about one's sense of self/identity.

- Identity alteration or a sense of acting like a different person.

Taken from: Marlene Steinberg. "In-Depth: Understanding Dissociative Disorders." Psych Central. http://psychcentral.com/lib/2008/in-depth-understanding-dissociative-disorders/all/1/.

Depersonalization disorder may also involve feelings of numbness or loss of emotional "aliveness."

Dissociative identity disorder (DID) is considered the most severe dissociative disorder and involves all of the major dissociative symptoms. People with this disorder have more than one personality state, and the personality state controlling the person's behavior changes from time to time. Often, a stressor will cause the change in personality state. The various personality states have separate names, temperaments, gestures, and vocabularies. This disorder is often associated with severe physical or sexual abuse, especially abuse during childhood. Women are diagnosed with this disorder more often than men.

> **FAST FACT**
>
> Researchers disagree about whether a tendency toward dissociative disorders is inherited.

DDNOS (Dissociative disorder not otherwise specified) is a diagnostic category ascribed to patients with dissociative symptoms that do not meet the full criteria for a specific dissociative disorder.

Treatments

Studies now suggest that treatment of a specific dissociation disorder should be based on whether or not the manifestations are considered as the compartmentalized type or the detachment type. Treatment recommendations for the compartmentalized types of disorders include focusing on reactivating and integrating the isolated mental compartments, possibly through hypnosis. To address detachment-based dissociation, therapies may include identifying triggers for the detached state, and determining how to stop the triggers and/or stop the detached condition when it is triggered. Standard approaches for these tactics may include cognitive-behavioral therapy.

Depersonalization Disorder Causes a Person to Feel Detached from Self

Batul Nafisa Baxamusa

In the following viewpoint the author explains that depersonalization disorder is a condition in which a person feels detached from his or her self, perhaps as if living in a dream or as if observing oneself from the outside. People with this disorder are fully aware that these feelings are not normal and that they have a mental problem of some kind. It can last a short time or for years, and it may cause serious interference with their social and professional lives. Treatment from a therapist can help to control the symptoms.

Batul Nafisa Baxamusa is a postgraduate student in hospital management as well as a writer who has published more than two thousand articles on the World Wide Web.

A strange affliction gripping your mind and soul. You seem lost in the world around you. One moment you were right there traveling in a bus to meet the love of your life. Suddenly, you feel changes occurring around you. The coffee table where you met your love for *the first time seems, different. . . . You do not belong here, as if you are a lost traveler in a strange land. Wait . . . there are a string of thoughts running through your mind. These thoughts aren't yours, this is an unreal situation. The inner world and outer world both appear unknown. Emotions? They appear so empty, so dead. Or is it a rush of emotions flowing right through your body? Insanity or a dream, this depersonalization disorder is pushing you, and [your] entire life, over the edge of a deep [abyss] that has no end.*

What Is Depersonalization Disorder?

Depersonalization disorder is a period of disconnect or detachment a person has from his/her body and thoughts. It causes one to feel as if they are living a dream and are detached from themselves. This episode of depersonalization episode may last for a few minutes, hours, and in some cases for years. The comorbidity [coexisting conditions] of depersonalization disorder includes obsessive-compulsive disorder, panic disorder, major depression. The characteristic sign of depersonalization disorder is that the person is totally aware that he/she is not an automaton. They are aware of the reality that the sensations and feelings experienced by them are not true.

The person experiencing depersonalization suffers from misinterpretation of the thoughts and senses. They often talk about a 'out-of-body' experience. The depersonalization disorder belongs to a group of dissociative disorders. These disorders are mostly mental illnesses that cause a person to suffer from memory disruptions, loss of consciousness or awareness about the surroundings, change in mental perception as well as personality. These disruptions and breakdowns cause interference with the daily functioning, professional, social and personal relationship of the depersonalized individual.

It is very hard to pinpoint the exact cause of depersonalization disorder. It is thought an emotional trauma that may have occurred in childhood may trigger depersonalization. In some cases, severe mental stress, major depressive disorder, hallucinogen ingestion and panic attacks are found to be the common causes for depersonalization disorder. It is very rare to observe depersonalization occur as an individual disorder. People who have been through a traumatic attack, accident or illness have been found to suffer from this disorder.

Symptoms

The main symptom of depersonalization disorder is alteration of mental perception. The person begins to feel as if they are living in a dream or some kind of a movie. They are under the impression that they are just an observer of their thoughts, their body and themselves. These people have a 'out-of-the-body' experience and form a numb feeling towards the world around them. A sudden sensation grips the mind as if they are not in control of their actions as well as the ability to speak. Some people begin to hallucinate that their body parts have grown abnormally large or shrunk down to a miniature size. Many have a feeling of floating in the air and observing themselves on the ground. These episodes also cause a person to have an emotional disconnect from the people around them. These episodes may last for a few hours, days or months and even years at a time, thus causing a lot of problems in the professional as well as personal life of that person.

The person experiencing depersonalization is well aware of the fact that he/she is suffering from some kind of mental problem. Thus, it is easier for one to seek psychological help from a mental health professional. There are certain depersonalization disorder tests conducted by psychologist that helps them diagnose the condition to understand different illnesses. These illnesses include borderline personality disorder or dissociative disorders.

FAST FACT

According to the International Society for the Study of Trauma and Dissociation, researchers estimate that depersonalization disorder is the third most common psychological disorder, following depression and anxiety.

The main symptom of depersonalization disorder is an altered state of perception in which one feels like one is living in a dream or a movie. (© Jean-Françoise Podevin/ Photo Researchers, Inc.)

Treatment

The treatment for depersonalization disorder includes a combination of therapies like psychotherapy and cognitive therapy. Clinical hypnosis also helps in some cases. A group therapy with the family helps the members of the family understand and spot the signs of depersonalization. There are no specific medications for depersonalization treatment. However, medications like antidepressants, antianxiety medications etc. help in overcoming the feelings of depression and anxiety.

Overcoming depersonalization disorder will help control the symptoms that trigger stress and trauma in the person experiencing it. Treatment will help control the underlying problems that trigger a depersonalization episode. One may not be able to prevent depersonalization disorder, but can always control the symptoms with treatment.

Dissociative Fugue Is Amnesia Combined with Sudden Travel Away from Home

Sulav Shrestha

Dissociative fugue is a rare disorder in which a person suddenly travels a long distance, having forgotten his or her identity and where home is, explains Sulav Shrestha in the following viewpoint. This amnesia may last only a few hours or it may persist for months, during which the person may adopt a new identity or be dazed and confused. If identified by others, someone in a fugue state may not recognize them. Fugue is caused by some form of stress and is more common after natural disasters. People may recover spontaneously or they may need psychotherapy. After recovery, their older memories return, but they lose all memory of what happened during the fugue period.

Sulav Shrestha is a medical student who blogs about medicine. He lives in Kathmandu, Nepal.

SOURCE: Sulav Shrestha, "Dissociative Fugue: 'Lost,'" Medchrome .com, May 7, 2011. Copyright © 2011 by Medchrome. All rights reserved. Reproduced by permission.

Dissociative fugue, formerly called psychogenic fugue, is a rare condition characterized by sudden, unexpected travel away from home or one's customary place of work, with inability to recall one's past, confusion about personal identity, or the assumption of a new identity, or significant distress or impairment. It is one of the least understood and yet clinically one of the most fascinating disorders in mental health.

The word fugue comes from the Latin word for "flight." The travels associated with the condition can last for a few hours or as long as several months. People experiencing dissociative fugue may be easily able to blend in wherever they end up. Initially, a person experiencing the condition may appear completely normal but with time, however, the victim realizes something is wrong. After recovery from fugue, previous memories usually return intact, but there is complete amnesia for the fugue episode.

Commonly, individuals who experience the onset of dissociative fugue are found wandering in a dazed or confused state, unable to recall their own identity or recognize their own relatives or daily surroundings. Often, the fugue state remains undiagnosed until the individual has emerged from it and can recall their real identity. It is estimated to affect just 0.2% of the population, nearly all of them adults.

Dissociative fugue must not be confused with Dissociative Identity Disorder, Wanderlust and Malingering [feigning illness to avoid work or other tasks].

FAST FACT

According to the Cleveland Clinic, art therapy and music therapy may be used in patients with dissociative fugue to help them express themselves in a safe way.

Causes of Dissociative Fugue

- Severe stress associated with traumatic events like war, abuse, accidents, disasters or extreme violence.
- Major life stresses (abandonment, death of a loved one, financial troubles)

• Tremendous internal conflict (turmoil over guilt-ridden impulses, apparently unresolvable interpersonal difficulties, criminal behaviors).

The frequency of dissociative fugue tends to increase during stressful or traumatic periods, such as during wartime or after a natural disaster.

Signs and Symptoms

• Sudden and unplanned travel away from home
• Inability to recall past events or important information from the person's life
• Confusion or loss of memory about his or her identity, possibly assuming a new identity to make up for the loss
• Patient may present alert and oriented only to self.

- Reasoning and judgment are lacking, and insight is poor.
- An increased finding of violent or homicidal ideation [thoughts] is present, but suicidal ideation is lacking.

Unconscious Knowledge of a Language in a Fugue Patient Who Could No Longer Speak It

Researchers gave tests to a man with dissociative fugue who could not remember his native language, which was German. He was shown pairs of German/English words—some related, some unrelated, and some that were not real German words—and asked to recall the second word of the pair he had just seen. The same test was given to two other people, one who knew only English and one who also knew German. The graph shows that he had some unconscious knowledge of it compared to a person who knew no German, even though he did not recognize many of the German words that were not related to the English ones.

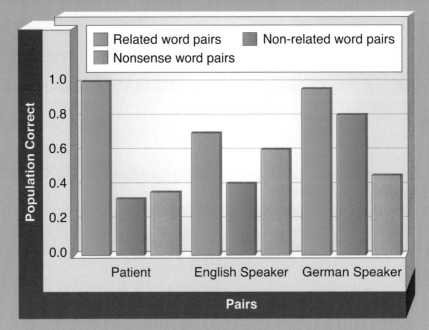

Taken from: Elizabeth L. Gliksy et al. "A Case of Psychogenic Fugue: I Understand, aber ich verstehe nichts." *Neuropsychologia* 42 (2004) 1132–1147. www.buedu/brainlab/files/2011/01/Gliksy.Ryan_.Hayes_.2003. PsychogenicFugue.Neuropsychologia.pdf.

Patients with dissociative fugue often recover spontaneously. However treatment involves:

- Psychotherapy with additional hypnosis and psychopharmacology in order to allow integration of feelings, anxieties associated with the fugue, and recovery techniques
- Medication and cognitive therapies in combination.

. . .

Real-Life Story of Dissociative Fugue

Jeffrey Alan Ingram, 40, was diagnosed in Denver with dissociative fugue, a type of amnesia.

When Jeff Ingram realized he did not belong in Denver he made public appeals on TV programs for anyone who might know his identity. His fiancé's brother saw him and called her. Two Denver police detectives accompanied him on a flight back to Olympia, Washington to be reunited with Penny. He had previous episodes in 1995, disappearing for 9 months, ending up in a Seattle hospital. This time (September, 06) he started a trip to Alberta, Canada to visit a friend dying of cancer.

He had awoken in Denver with $8 and no memory of how he got there or who he was. He wandered the streets until he was picked up and placed in a hospital for testing. His memories of the former life are all missing. His car, a greenish-blue colored Neon, is still missing. The ability to cook is gone as well as his driving skills.

Experts insist the stress of dealing with a friend's pending death caused the fugue episode.

In People with Dissociative Identity Disorder, Separate Personalities Alternate

Veronica Pamoukaghlian

According to the author of this viewpoint, dissociative identity disorder (DID) is more complex than it is shown to be by the media, which do not always treat it seriously. It is generally developed as a response to trauma such as early childhood abuse, when instead of dissociating belief, which would be useful, a person escapes by creating new alternate personas (alters) that exist along with his or her original one and periodically assume control. Diagnosis of DID is difficult and often takes a long time. Though some alters are harmless, there is a risk of some causing harm to other people, or of suicide, and DID patients have been convicted of crime without being aware that it was committed by an alter. Studies have shown that some forms of treatment for DID are effective.

Veronica Pamoukaghlian is a Uruguayan writer, travel blogger, and filmmaker. She has directed two documentaries on psychiatric wards.

SOURCE: Veronica Pamoukaghlian, "Behind the Masks—The Mysteries of Dissociative Identity Disorder," BrainBlogger.com, August 2011. Copyright © 2011 by the Global Neuroscience Initiative Foundation. All rights reserved. Reproduced by permission.

While [actress] Toni Collette may have pulled off making dissociative identity disorder (DID) look glamorous and sexy in the recently cancelled Showtime series *United States of Tara*, the reality of this disorder is much more complex. As fun as it is to watch an actress play five different parts in one show, for people with DID, the shifting is no fun at all.

One thing the show did get right is the fact that most people with DID develop it as a response to trauma, especially early childhood abuse from a parent or caregiver; studies have consistently reported this in 95–98% of the cases. People develop this disorder in order to distance themselves from the traumatic experience, by way of creating other personalities. While momentary dissociation is a technique that normal people use to cope with traumatic situations, in the case of people with DID, this dissociation goes beyond the moment, creating a whole new persona that has not been affected by the abuse, as an escape mechanism.

The prevalence of DID in the general population has been established at 1%, making it far more common than popular belief would have it. Nevertheless, the allure of the "exotic" continues to surround this condition, for example, because hypnosis is commonly used to gain access to the alters, as the different personalities are called. A scientifically accepted technique, hypnosis still remains, in the public mind, a practice bordering the world of the occult, found more at home in magic shows than in the therapist's office.

Diagnosing DID

Perhaps because of its assumed rarity, it is the diagnosis of DID that poses one of the biggest problems. In 1993, a Dutch study of 71 DID patients established that: "Patients had spent an average of 8.2 years in the mental health system prior to correct diagnosis. Patients presented with many different symptoms and frequently received other psychiatric or neurological diagnoses."

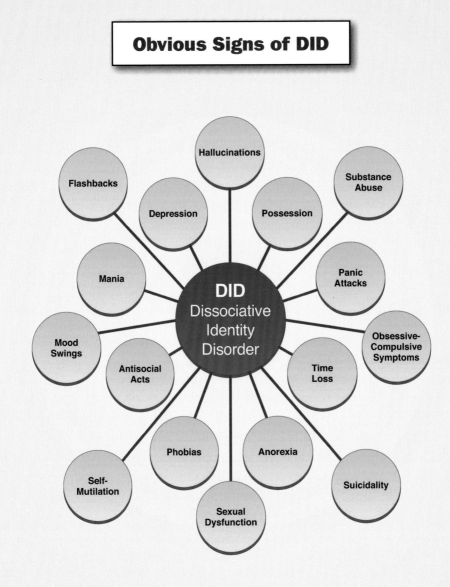

Obvious Signs of DID

Hallucinations

Flashbacks

Depression

Possession

Substance Abuse

Mania

DID
Dissociative Identity Disorder

Panic Attacks

Mood Swings

Antisocial Acts

Time Loss

Obsessive-Compulsive Symptoms

Phobias

Anorexia

Self-Mutilation

Sexual Dysfunction

Suicidality

Taken from: Marlene Steinberg. "In-Depth: Understanding Dissociative Disorders." Psych Central. http://psychcentral.com/lib/2008/in-depth-understanding-dissociative-disorders/all/1/.

Over the years, studies carried out in other parts of the world have yielded similar results, raising awareness about DID and the methods that could be used to identify it, separating it from other disorders, some of which can sometimes be comorbid with it, thus further complicating an effective diagnosis.

According to DSM IV [the fourth edition of the *Diagnostic and Statistical Manual of Mental Disorders*], DID can be diagnosed whenever there is a coexistence of:

- The presence of two or more distinct identities or personality states (each with its own relatively enduring pattern of perceiving, relating to, and thinking about the environment and self).
- At least two of these identity or personality states recurrently take control of the person's behavior.
- Inability to recall important personal information that is too extensive to be explained by ordinary forgetfulness and not due to the direct effects of a substance (e.g. blackouts or chaotic behaviour during alcohol intoxication) or a general medical condition (e.g. complex partial seizures).

Dangers of DID

While some alters can be harmless, a study on DID and suicidality found a strong correlation between the disorder and repeated suicide attempts, as well as the risk of causing harm to others. As the DID patient does not control the alters, this presents a great danger. In fact, DID patients have often been involved in crime investigations, and North American law has even recognized the right of the different personalities to have different attorneys, outlining a plot fit for the ultimate trial film from Hollywood. Courts have also been known to take the testimonies of the different alters as if they were actually different people, especially in cases in which one of the "bad" alters has committed a crime that neither the patient's main personality nor the other alters have a recollection of.

Many times, people have ended up going to jail for crimes committed by one of their alters. Even today, with

> **FAST FACT**
>
> In 1898 French psychologist Ludovic Dugar coined the term *depersonalization* to describe those experiencing symptoms involving loss of mental function.

Although actress Toni Collette in the TV show *United States of Tara* (shown here as one of her alters) made DID look fun and interesting, for real DID patients it is usually unpleasant and often scary. (© Dreamworks TV/ The Kobal Collection/ Althaus, Jordin/The Kobal Collection at Art Resource, NY)

all the developments and research carried out by the scientific community, it seems that DID remains as mysterious as ever, and people continue to suffer from this disorder without even being aware of it, all over the world.

For those who have been successfully diagnosed, the International Society for the Study of Dissociation (ISSD) has developed a phasic treatment framework for dissociation disorders, including DID. The three phases are:

- safety, stabilization and symptom reduction
- working directly and in depth with traumatic memories
- identity integration and rehabilitation

A recent study by DID expert Bethany Brand and some of her colleagues concluded, after analyzing most of the current literature and research pertaining to DID treatment results, that the three-phase treatment has been widely effective, bringing about a reduction of "symptoms of dissociation, depression, general distress, anxiety and PTSD [post-traumatic stress disorder]."

CHAPTER 2

Controversies Concerning Dissociative Disorders

Dissociative Identity Disorder Is Widely Misunderstood

Margarita Tartakovsky

In the following viewpoint Margarita Tartakovsky counters the misconception that dissociative identity disorder (DID), which was known previously as multiple personality disorder, is not a real disorder. DID is misunderstood, she argues, and there are many myths about it, due to a lack of information. The disorder is not as rare as is often thought, but it is usually not as obvious as media portrayals suggest. Critics say that therapy makes DID worse, but that is true only when therapists use outdated methods of treatment; proper treatment helps DID patients to gradually integrate their various states. Tartakovsky asserts that good therapists never use hypnosis to explore memories, since it has been found to create false memories; rather, it is used only to manage symptoms.

Tartakovsky is an associate editor at the website Psych Central.

Photo on previous page.
People with dissociative identity disorder
can have separate,
alternating personalities.
(© Alain Dex/Publiphoto/
Photo Researchers, Inc.)

Dissociative identity disorder (DID), known previously as multiple personality disorder, is not a real disorder. At least, that's what you might've heard in the media, and even from some mental health professionals. DID is arguably one of the most misunderstood and controversial diagnoses in the current *Diagnostic and Statistical Manual of Mental Disorders* (DSM). But it is a real and debilitating disorder that makes it difficult for people to function.

Why the Controversy?

According to Bethany Brand, Ph.D, a professor of psychology at Towson University and an expert in treating and researching dissociative disorders, there are several reasons. DID is associated with early severe trauma, such as abuse and neglect.

This raises the concern over false memories. Some people worry that clients may "remember" abuse that didn't actually happen and innocent people may get blamed for abuse. ("Most people with DID don't forget all their abuse or trauma," Brand said; "sufferers may forget episodes or aspects of some of their trauma," but it's "fairly rare not to remember any trauma at all and suddenly recover memories of chronic childhood abuse.") It also "pries into families' privacy," and families may be reluctant to reveal information that might put them in a negative light.

In the mental health field, myths persist because of a lack of education and training about DID. These myths create a mystique around the disorder and perpetuate the belief that DID is bizarre. For instance, one prevalent myth is that there are "different people inside someone with DID," Brand said. Adding to the problem are poorly trained therapists who promote atypical treatments that aren't supported by the expert clinical community. "Mainstream, well-trained dissociative experts don't advocate using bizarre treatment interventions. Rather, they use interventions that are similar to common ones used in treating complex trauma," she said.

DID typically develops in childhood as a result of severe and sustained trauma. It's characterized by different identities or "self-states" (there is no integrated sense of self) and an inability to recall information that goes beyond forgetfulness. Prone to amnesia, people with DID sometimes "can't remember what they've done or said," Brand said. They have a tendency to dissociate or "space out and lose track of minutes or hours." For instance, it's "common [for people with DID] to find they've hurt themselves [but] don't remember doing that," Brand said. The loss of memory isn't due to drugs or alcohol, but a switch in self-states, she noted. . . .

Seven Common DID Myths

It's safe to say that most of what we know about DID is either exaggerated or flat-out false. Here's a list of common myths, followed by the facts.

1. DID is rare. Studies show that in the general population about 1 to 3 percent meet full criteria for DID. This makes the disorder as common as bipolar disorder and schizophrenia. The rates in clinical populations are even higher, Brand said. Unfortunately, even though DID is fairly common, research about it is grossly underfunded. Researchers often use their own money to fund studies or volunteer their time. (The National Institute of Mental Health has yet to fund a single treatment study on DID.)

2. It's obvious when someone has DID. Sensationalism sells. So it's not surprising that depictions of DID in movies and TV are exaggerated. The more bizarre the portrayal, the more it fascinates and tempts viewers to tune in. Also, overstated portrayals make it obvious that a person has DID. But "DID is much more subtle than any Hollywood portrayal," Brand said. In fact, people with DID spend an average of seven years in the mental health system before being diagnosed.

Psychologists are quick to point out that a child may have false memories of being abused.
(© Doug Martin/Photo Researchers, Inc.)

They also have comorbid [other, simultaneous] disorders, making it harder to identify DID. They often struggle with severe treatment-resistant depression, post-traumatic stress disorder (PTSD), eating disorders and substance abuse. Because standard treatment for these disorders doesn't treat the DID, these individuals don't get much better, Brand said.

3. People with DID have distinct personalities. Instead of distinct personalities, people with DID have different states. Brand describes it as "having different ways of being themselves, which we all do to some extent, but people with DID cannot always recall what they do or say while in their different states." And they may act quite differently in different states.

Also, "There are many disorders that involve changes in state." For instance, people with borderline personality disorder may go "from relatively calm to extremely angry with little provocation." People with panic disorder may go "from an even emotional state to extremely panicked." "However, patients with those disorders recall what they do and say in these different states, in contrast to the occasional amnesia that DID patients experience."

As Brand points out, in the media, there is a great fascination with the self-states. But the self-states are not the biggest focus in treatment. Therapists address clients' severe depression, dissociation, self-harm, painful memories and overwhelming feelings. They also help individuals "modulate their impulses" in all their states. The "majority [of treatment] is much more mundane than Hollywood would lead us to expect," Brand said.

4. Treatment makes DID worse. Some critics of DID believe that treatment exacerbates the disorder. It's true that misinformed therapists who use outdated or ineffective approaches may do damage. But this can happen with any disorder with any inexperienced and ill-trained therapist. Research-based and consensually established treatments for DID do help.

The International Society for The Study of Trauma and Dissociation, the premier organization that trains therapists to assess and treat dissociative disorders, features the latest adult treatment guidelines on their homepage. These guidelines, which Brand helped co-author, are based on up-to-date research and clinical experience. (The website also offers guidelines for kids and teens with dissociative disorders.)

Brand and colleagues recently conducted a review of treatment studies on dissociative disorders, which was published in the *Journal of Nervous Mental Disease.* While the reviewed studies have limitations—no control or comparison groups and small sample sizes—results revealed that individuals do get better. Specifically, the authors found improvements in dissociative symptoms,

FAST FACT

Multiple personalities (alters) of the same person often have noticeable differences not only in behavior but in their voices, mannerisms, and physical attributes. For example, one alter may need glasses when another does not.

depression, distress, anxiety, PTSD and work and social functioning. More research is needed. Brand along with colleagues from the U.S. and abroad are working on a larger scale study to test treatment outcomes.

5. *Therapists further develop and "reify" (regard them as real or concrete) the self-states.* Quite the opposite, therapists try to create an "inner communication and co-operation among self-states," Brand said. They teach patients to manage their feelings, impulses and memories. This is especially important because a person switches self-states when they're faced with overwhelming memories or feelings such as fear and anger.

Therapists help patients integrate their states, which is a process that happens over time. Unlike movies and media depict, integration isn't "a big dramatic event," Brand said. Instead eventually, the differences among states diminish, and the person is better able to handle strong feelings and memories without switching self-states and retreating from reality.

6. *Only people with DID dissociate.* People dissociate in response to trauma or other overwhelming situations such as intense pain or anxiety. So individuals with other disorders such as anxiety disorders and PTSD also dissociate. (In about six months a journal that specializes in depression and anxiety will focus its entire issue on dissociation.)

Researchers in other fields, specifically PTSD, are starting to reanalyze their data and categorize individuals into high dissociatives and low dissociatives. They're learning that people who are high dissociatives often have a slower or poorer response to treatment. This shows that much more research is needed to learn how to better treat dissociative individuals, Brand said.

Also, brain studies have shown that high dissociatives exhibit different brain activity than low dissociatives. A 2010 review in *The American Journal of Psychiatry* concluded that people who have the dissociative subtype of

PTSD "tend to have less activation in the emotional centers of the brain while recalling their traumas and while dissociating than do people with classic PTSD."

7. Hypnosis is used to access or explore hidden memories. Some therapists used to believe that hypnosis could help clients retrieve accurate memories (like memories of abuse). Now, compelling research has shown that "experiences recalled under hypnosis can feel very true," even though the person never experienced these events, Brand said. She added that all the reputable professional associations that provide training in hypnosis "educated therapists that they should never use hypnosis to try and facilitate recall of memory." So if a therapist says they use hypnosis to explore memories, Brand underscored the importance of obtaining information about their trauma training.

Well-trained therapists use hypnosis only to manage common symptoms such as anxiety and chronic pain. People with DID tend to struggle with insomnia, and hypnosis improves sleep. It also "helps contain PTSD flashbacks," and provides "distance from and control over traumatic, intrusive memories," Brand said. People with DID often experience severe migraines, which may be "correlated with internal conflict amongst personality states." For instance, one self-state may want to commit suicide while the others don't.

Chronic health problems are common among people with DID. The underlying reason may be stress. The ACE studies have found a link between "adverse childhood events (ACE)" like parents' substance abuse and divorce, as well as childhood abuse, and various psychological and medical problems.

Brand uses hypnosis in her sessions, which she describes as "facilitating a positive change in state of consciousness." Many people with DID are actually highly hypnotizable, she said. To hypnotize a client, Brand simply says: "I want you to breathe slowly and deeply and imagine being in a safe place."

A Sample DID Case

So what does DID look like? According to Brand, picture a middle-aged woman who's been in the mental health system for about 10 years. She comes into therapy seeking help for her self-destructive behaviors. She cuts herself, has made several suicide attempts and struggles with a disabling depression. She never mentions having DID. (Most people with DID don't realize they have it, or if they do, they keep it hidden because they don't want to be seen as "crazy.")

But she's aware that she "loses" gaps of time and has a bad memory. During sessions with her therapist, she spaces out. Often the therapist has to call her name to bring her back to the present. People have occasionally mentioned her out-of-character behavior. For instance, even though she rarely drinks, she's been told that at times, she drinks a lot of alcohol. She realizes that this must be true because she's felt hungover before but couldn't remember having a single drink. "However, she admits only to herself that she cannot recall what she did for several hours on the nights before the hangovers. She tries not to think about these unexplained, frightening experiences."

She also experiences PTSD-like symptoms. She recalls being choked and sometimes coughs profusely and feels like she can't catch her breath. Or she gags when brushing her teeth. She struggles with a poor body image, low self-esteem and a number of chronic health problems, including fibromyalgia and migraines.

(Keep in mind this example contains generalizations.)

Regardless of the controversy, dissociative identity disorder is a real disorder that disrupts people's lives. But there is hope and help.

Some Psychologists Disagree with the Prevailing View of Dissociative Identity Disorder

Robert T. Carroll

According to the author of the following viewpoint, some psychologists believe that there is a better explanation for multiple personality disorder (MPD)—now called dissociative identity disorder—than the prevalent theory that assumes a person has hidden alternate personalities resulting from childhood abuse. Rather, they say, the disorder is created by the expectations of the doctors who treat it, and of society. Although it seems incredible that this could be happening, something similar happened in the past: Society believed behavior caused by brain damage or physical disease was caused by demons, which seemed entirely real to people of that time, including the patients, but is rarely considered real today. In the same way, relates the author, MPD patients unconsciously learn to act according to what is believed about multiplicity, which is different from what is believed in other cultures. But defenders of the standard medical mode of MPD are unlikely to change their views, and in any case, the suffering of people with MPD is real.

Robert T. Carroll is a retired teacher of philosophy at Sacramento City College. He is the author of several books, including *The Skeptic's Dictionary*.

Students often ask me whether multiple personality disorder (MPD) really exists. I usually reply that the symptoms attributed to it are as genuine as hysterical paralysis and seizures.

—Dr. Paul McHugh

Multiple personality disorder (MPD) is a psychiatric disorder characterized by having at least one "alter" personality that controls behavior. The "alters" are said to occur spontaneously and involuntarily, and function more or less independently of each other. The unity of consciousness, by which we identify our selves, is said to be absent in MPD. Many labeled with MPD seek mental health treatment programs to help manage the disorder. Another symptom of MPD is significant amnesia which can't be explained by ordinary forgetfulness. In 1994, the American Psychiatric Association's DSM-IV [*Diagnostic and Statistical Manual of Mental Disorders*, 4th ed.] replaced the designation of MPD with DID: *dissociative identity disorder*. The label may have changed, but the list of symptoms remained essentially the same.

Memory and other aspects of consciousness are said to be divided up among "alters" in the MPD. The number of "alters" identified by various therapists ranges from several to tens to hundreds. There are even some reports of several thousand identities dwelling in one person. There does not seem to be any consensus among therapists as to what an "alter" is. Yet, there is general agreement that the cause of MPD is repressed memories of childhood sexual abuse. The evidence for this claim has been challenged, however, and there are very few reported cases of MPD afflicting children.

Psychologist Nicholas P. Spanos argues that repressed memories of childhood abuse and multiple personality disorder are "rule-governed social constructions established, legitimated, and maintained through social interaction." In short, Spanos argues that most cases of MPD have been created by therapists with the cooperation of their patients and the rest of society. The experts have created both the disease and the cure. This does not mean that MPD does not exist, but that its origin and development are often, if not most often, explicable without the model of separate but permeable ego-states or "alters" arising out of the ashes of a destroyed "original self."

Explaining MPD

A rather common view of MPD is given by philosopher Daniel Dennett:

> The evidence is now voluminous that there are not a handful or a hundred but thousands of cases of MPD diagnosed today, and it almost invariably owes its existence to prolonged early childhood abuse, usually sexual, and of sickening severity. Nicholas Humphrey and I investigated MPD several years ago and found it to be a complex phenomenon that extends far beyond individual brains and the sufferers.

These children have often been kept in such extraordinary terrifying and confusing circumstances that I am more amazed that they survive psychologically at all than I am that they manage to preserve themselves by a desperate redrawing of their boundaries. What they do, when confronted with overwhelming conflict and pain, is this: They "leave." They create a boundary so that the horror doesn't happen to them; it either happens to no one, or to some other self, better able to sustain its organization under such an onslaught—at least that's what they say they did, as best they recall.

Dennett exhibits minimal skepticism about the truth of the MPD accounts, and focuses on how they can be explained metaphysically and biologically. For all his brilliant exploration of the concept of the self, the one perspective he doesn't seem to give much weight to is the one Spanos takes: that the self and the multiple selves of the

MPD patient are social constructs, not needing a meta-physical or biological explanation so much as a social-psychological one. That is not to say that our biology is not a significant determining factor in the development of our ideas about selves, including our own self. It is to say, however, that before we go off worrying about how to metaphysically explain one or a hundred selves in one body, or one self in a hundred bodies, we might want to consider that a phenomenological analysis of behavior which takes that behavior at face value, or which attributes it to nothing but brain structure and biochemistry, may be missing the most significant element in the creation of the self: the sociocognitive context in which our

Coexisting Diagnoses or Misdiagnoses Often Applied to People with DID

- Major depression
- Generalized anxiety disorder
- Bipolar disorder
- Attention deficit/hyperactivity disorder
- Obsessive-compulsive disorder
- Eating disorders
- Substance-abuse disorders
- Sleep disorders
- Impulse-control disorders

Taken from: Marlene Steinberg. "In-Depth: Understanding Dissociative Disorders." Psych Central. http://psychcentral.com/lib/2008/in-depth-understanding-dissociative-disorders/all/1/.

ideas of self, disease, personality, memory, etc., emerge. Being a social construct does not make the self any less real, by the way. And Spanos should not be taken to deny either that the self exists or that MPD exists.

But if thinkers of Dennett's stature accept MPD as something which needs explaining in terms of psychological dynamics limited to the psyche of the abused rather than in terms of social constructs, the task of convincing therapists who treat MPD to accept Spanos' way of thinking is Herculean. How could it be possible that most MPD patients have been created in the therapist's laboratory, so to speak? How could it be possible that so many people, particularly female people (85% of MPD patients are female), could have so many false memories of childhood sexual abuse? How could so many people behave as if their bodies have been invaded by numerous entities or personalities, if they hadn't really been so invaded? How could so many people actually experience past lives under hypnosis, a standard procedure of some therapists who treat MPD? How could the defense mechanism explanation for MPD, in terms of repression of childhood sexual trauma and dissociation, not be correct? How could so many people be so wrong about so much? Spanos' answer makes it sound almost too easy for such a massive amount of self-deception and delusion to develop: it's happened before and we all know about it. Remember demonic possession?

> ## FAST FACT
>
> People with dissociative identity disorder often have other mental disorders, too, so their dissociation may not be detected.

Comparison with Demonic Possession

Most educated people today do not try to explain epilepsy, brain damage, genetic disorders, neurochemical imbalances, feverish hallucinations, or troublesome behavior by appealing to the idea of demonic possession. Yet, at one time, all of Europe and America would have accepted such an explanation. Furthermore, we had our experts—the priests and theologians—to tell us how to identify the possessed and how to exorcise the demons. An elaborate theological framework bolstered this world-view, and an elaborate set of social rituals and behaviors validated it on a continuous basis. In fact, every culture, no matter how primitive and pre-scientific, had a belief in some form of demonic possession. It had its shamans and witch doctors who performed rituals to rid the possessed of their demons. In their own sociocognitive contexts, such beliefs and behaviors were seen as obviously correct, and were constantly reinforced by traditional and customary social behaviors and expectations.

Most educated people today believe that the behaviors of witches and other possessed persons—as well as the behaviors of their tormentors, exorcists, and executioners—were enactments of social roles. With the exception of religious fundamentalists (who still live in the world of demons, witches, and supernatural magic), educated people do not believe that in those days there really were witches, or that demons really did invade bodies, or that priests really did exorcise those demons by their ritualistic magic. Yet, for those who lived in the time of witches and demons, these beings were as real as anything else they experienced. In Spanos' view, what is true of the world of demons and exorcists is true of the psychological world filled with phenomena such as repression of childhood sexual trauma and its manifestation in such disorders as MPD.

Spanos makes a very strong case for the claim that "patients learn to construe themselves as possessing multiple selves, learn to present themselves in terms of this construal, and learn to reorganize and elaborate on their personal biography so as to make it congruent with their understanding of what it means to be a multiple." Psychotherapists, according to Spanos, "play a particularly important part in the generation and maintenance of MPD." According to Spanos, most therapists never see a single case of MPD and some therapists report seeing hundreds of cases each year. It should be distressing to those trying to defend the integrity of psychotherapy that a patient's diagnosis depends upon the preconceptions of the therapist. However, an MPD patient typically has no memory of sexual abuse upon entering therapy. Only after the therapist encourages the patient do memories of sexual abuses emerge. Furthermore, the typical MPD patient does not begin manifesting "alters" until *after* treatment begins. MPD therapists counter these charges by claiming that their methods are tried and true, which they know from experience, and those therapists who never treat MPD don't know what to look for.

Multiple selves exist, and have existed in other cultures, without being related to the notion of a mental disorder, as is the case today in North America. According to Spanos, "Multiple identities can develop in a wide

Dissociative identity disorder is characterized by having at least one alter personality that controls behavior.
(© John Oeth/Alamy)

variety of cultural contexts and serve numerous different social functions." Neither childhood sexual abuse nor mental disorder is a necessary condition for multiple personality to manifest itself. Multiple personalities are best understood as "rule-governed social constructions." They "are established, legitimated, maintained, and altered through social interaction." In a number of different historical and social contexts, people have learned to think of themselves as "possessing more than one identity or self, and can learn to behave as if they are first one identity and then a different identity." However, "people are unlikely to think of themselves in this way or to behave in this way unless their culture has provided models from whom the rules and characteristics of multiple identity enactments can be learned. Along with providing rules and models, the culture, through its socializing agents, must also provide legitimation for multiple self enactments." Again, Spanos is not saying that MPD does not exist, but that the standard model of (a) *abuse,* (b) *withdrawal of original self,* and then (c) *emergence of alters,* is not needed to explain MPD. Nor is the psychological baggage that goes with that model: repression, recovered memory of childhood sexual abuse, integration of alters in therapy. Nor are the standard diagnostic techniques: hypnosis, including past life regression, and Rorschach tests.

Influence of Books and Movies

It should be noted that books and films have had a strong influence on the belief in the nature of MPD, e.g., *Sybil, The Three Faces of Eve, The Five of Me,* or *The Minds of Billy Milligan.* These mass media presentations influence not only the general public's beliefs about MPD, but they affect MPD patients as well. For example, Flora Rheta Schreiber's *Sybil* is the story of a woman with sixteen personalities allegedly created in response to having been abused as a child. Before the publication of *Sybil* in

1973 and the 1976 television movie starring Sally Fields as Sybil, there had been only about 75 reported cases of MPD. Since *Sybil* there have some 40,000 diagnoses of MPD, mostly in North America.

Sybil has been identified as Shirley Ardell Mason, who died of breast cancer in 1998 at the age of 75. Her therapist has been identified as Cornelia Wilbur, who died in 1992, leaving Mason $25,000 and all future royalties from *Sybil.* Schreiber died in 1988. It is now known that Mason had no MPD symptoms before therapy with Wilbur, who used hypnosis and other suggestive techniques to tease out the so-called "personalities." *Newsweek* reports that, according to historian Peter M. Swales (who first identified Mason as Sybil), "there is strong evidence that [the worst abuse in the book] could not have happened."

Dr. Herbert Spiegel, who also treated "Sybil", believes Wilbur suggested the personalities as part of her therapy and that the patient adopted them with the help of hypnosis and sodium pentothal. He describes his patient as highly hypnotizable and extremely suggestible. Mason was so helpful that she read the literature on MPD, including *The Three Faces of Eve.* The Sybil episode seems clearly to be symptomatic of an iatrogenic [resulting from treatment] disorder. Yet, the Sybil case is the paradigm for the standard model of MPD. A defender of this model, Dr. Philip M. Coons, claims that "the relationship of multiple personality to child abuse was not generally recognized until the publication of Sybil."

The MPD community suffered another serious attack on its credibility when Dr. Bennett Braun, the founder of the International Society for the Study of Disassociation, had his license suspended over allegations he used drugs and hypnosis to convince a patient she killed scores of people in Satanic rituals. The patient claims that Braun convinced her that she had 300 personalities, among them a child molester, a high priestess of a satanic cult, and a cannibal. The patient told the *Chicago Tribune:* "I began to add a few things up and realized there was no way I could come from a little town in Iowa, be eating 2,000 people a year, and nobody said anything about it." The patient won $10.6 million in a lawsuit against Braun, Rush–Presbyterian–St. Luke's Hospital, and another therapist.

Defenders of MPD

The defenders of the MPD/DID standard model of genesis, diagnosis, and treatment argue that the disease is underdiagnosed because its complexity makes it very difficult to identify. Dr. Philip M. Coons, who is in the Department of Psychiatry at the Indiana University School of Medicine, claims that "there is a professional reluctance to diagnose multiple personality disorder." He thinks this "stems from a number of factors including the generally subtle presentation of the symptoms, the fearful reluctance of the patient to divulge important clinical information, professional ignorance concerning dissociative disorders, and the reluctance of the clinician to believe that incest actually occurs and is not the product of fantasy." Dr. Coons also claims that demonic possession was "a forerunner of multiple personality."

Another defender of the standard model of MPD, Dr. Ralph Allison, has posted his diagnosis of Kenneth Bianchi, the so-called Hillside Strangler, in which the therapist admits he has changed his mind several times. Bianchi, now a convicted serial killer serving a life sentence, was diagnosed as having MPD by defense psychiatrist Jack G. Watkins. Dr. Watkins used hypnosis on Bianchi and "Steve" emerged to an explicit suggestion from the therapist. "Steve" was allegedly Bianchi's alter who did the murders. Prosecution psychiatrist Martin T. Orne, an expert on hypnosis, argued successfully before the court that the hypnosis and the MPD symptoms were a sham.

Allison claims, but offers no evidence, that the controversy over MPD is one between therapists, who defend the standard model, and teachers, who deny MPD exists.

The battle took place in committee when preparing the DSM-IV, he claims. The teachers won and MPD was removed and DID replaced it. The DSM-IV is the current version (1994) of the American Psychiatric Association's *Diagnostic & Statistical Manual of Mental Disorders*. It lists 410 mental disorders, up from 145 in DSM-II (1968). The first edition in 1952 listed 60 disorders. Some claim that this proliferation of disorders indicates an attempt of therapists to expand their market; others see the rise in disorders as evidence of better diagnostic tools. According to Allison, MPD was called "Hysterical Dissociative Disorder" in DSM-II and did not have its own code number. MPD was listed and coded in DSM-III, but removed in DSM-IV and replaced with DID.

It is possible, of course, that some cases of MPD emerge spontaneously without input from the MPD community, while other cases—perhaps most cases—of MPD have been created by therapists with the cooperation of their patients who have been influenced by authors and film makers. In either case, the suffering of the person with MPD is equally pitiable and deserving of our understanding, not derision.

Finally, there are some MPs who do not consider their condition to be a disorder, and whose main suffering comes from the thought of what others will think or do if they find out. They consider just about everything presented above from the psychiatrists, psychologists, philosophers, and other professionals to be myths. Like the fantasizing women in [Sheryl] Wilson and [Theodore] Barber's study of "fantasy-prone persons," there are many MPs who don't reveal their "secret" for fear of ridicule and ostracism.

The Assumptions of Dissociative Identity Disorder Proponents Have Been Scientifically Discredited

Carol Tavris

In the following viewpoint Carol Tavris explains that the phenomenal rise in multiple personality diagnoses (MPD, now called dissociative identity disorder, or DID) during the last two decades of the twentieth century, before which there had been only a few cases, was a result of social hysteria following the publication of *Sybil*, a best-selling book and later a television special. It has now been found that this book was a fabrication—the real "Sybil" lied to her psychotherapist; the psychotherapist knew this, and so did the book's author. Moreover, says Tavris, her symptoms corresponded to a physical disease with which she had been diagnosed. Yet now, even though some psychiatrists have been sued for inducing alleged multiple personalities in their patients, the majority continue to maintain that DID is a real disorder arising from childhood abuse.

Tavris is an eminent social psychologist and prolific author.

One of the most foolish and devastating episodes of social hysteria in America was the rise of "multiple personality disorder" in the era between, roughly, 1980 and 2000. Before 1980, only a handful of cases had ever existed world-wide, and the "multiples" came in pairs. In the 1950s, *The Three Faces of Eve* added one more personality to the mix. MPD then languished, as a rare psychiatric curiosity, until *Sybil* was published in 1973. The title patient produced 16 personalities before she was through, and became a national phenomenon. Flora Rheta Schreiber's book sold more than six million copies, and 40 million Americans watched the 1976 two-part television special starring Joanne Woodward and Sally Field.

If Helen's face launched a thousand ships, Sybil's faces launched tens of thousands. In her wake, people began coming out of therapy claiming that they had dozens, even hundreds, of "alters"—human, animal, mechanical and vegetable. By 1980 so many psychiatrists had begun looking for sensational cases of MPD in their own troubled clients—and finding them—that for the first time it became an official diagnosis in the *Diagnostic and Statistical Manual of Mental Disorders*. MPD was a growth industry; eminent hospitals, notably Rush Presbyterian in Chicago, opened MPD treatment centers. By the mid-1990s, according to some estimates, as many as 40,000 cases had been reported.

Yet Sybil's story, which started it all, was a complete fabrication. Sybil, whose real name was Shirley Mason, did not have a childhood trauma that caused her personality to fragment, and her "personalities" were largely generated in response to pressures, subtle and coercive, by her psychiatrist, Cornelia (Connie) Wilbur, whom she wanted desperately to please.

The true story of Sybil has found its ideal historian in Debbie Nathan, whose earlier book, *Satan's Silence* (with Michael Snedeker), debunked the "ritual sex abuse" panic that swept across the United States at the same time

A moment ago she was the nicest girl in town . . .
A moment from now she will be anybody's pick-up!

The Three Faces of Eve

CINEMASCOPE

JOANNE WOODWARD · DAVID WAYNE · LEE J. COBB · NUNNALLY JOHNSON

as MPD. Ms. Nathan's indefatigable detective work in "Sybil Exposed" has produced a major contribution to the history of psychiatric fads and the social manufacture of mental disorders. *This* is the book that should be a made-for-TV movie.

Self-Deception

Sybil was a fake, but not entirely a fraud. Self-deception, Ms. Nathan shows, was the motivation for all three principals involved in the creation of her persona: the patient, the psychiatrist and the writer. Each faced a choice when confronted with the evidence that Sybil was not a multiple personality: Accept the truth or press forward with a story they knew was a lie. Ms. Nathan deftly shows how emotional dependence, grandiose ambition and financial incentives from need to greed tilted their decisions.

Movies about multiple personality disorder, like *The Three Faces of Eve,* have had a strong influence on the general public's understanding of the disorder. (© 20th Century Fox/The Kobal Collection at Art Resource, NY)

Ms. Nathan begins with the early lives of the three: Shirley, who grew up in a tiny Minnesota town, the only child of Seventh-day Adventists; Connie, who saw wealth and professional glory if she could get a good story out of her distressed, dependent patient; and Flora, a New York magazine writer whom Connie commissioned to turn Shirley's story into a book with a "happy ending."

Each of these women, who came of age in the 1920s and 1930s, yearned to break out of the confines imposed on them by religion, region or gender: Shirley, to become an art teacher; Connie, to prove wrong her father's claim that she was "too stupid" to be a doctor or chemist; Flora, to become a great writer.

Shirley, who suffered from various physical and emotional ailments for most of her life, began psychoanalytic treatment with Connie in 1955. Before long, the two women struck a deal: Shirley would allow Connie to publish her story of being a multiple personality, and the cost of her treatment would be taken out of the book's royalties.

Connie began injecting Shirley with sodium pentothal (falsely called "truth serum," more properly "fanciful imaginings serum") and recording whatever Shirley said under its influence. Most of it was dreamlike garble, with an occasional alarming "memory" thrown in: Once Shirley recalled being forced onto a table, knocked out by medication and seeing a man looming above her. Connie assumed Shirley had been raped. Much later Shirley admitted it was a memory of her tonsillectomy. Maintaining the Lie Connie turned Shirley into an addict, giving her nearly a dozen drugs, including barbiturates, tranquilizers and anti-psychotics (such as Thorazine). Even with this "help," Ms. Nathan writes, "Shirley's new 'trauma' memories were pathetical-

FAST FACT

"A good rule of thumb is that any condition that has become a favorite with Hollywood, Oprah, and checkout-counter newspapers and magazines stands a great chance of being wildly overdiagnosed," says psychiatrists Allen Frances and Michael First—the chairperson and editor of the DSM-IV—in *Your Mental Health: A Layman's Guide to the Psychiatrist's Bible.*

ly trivial." But if Shirley couldn't produce a traumatic secret that was the reason for all her alters, there could be no resolution and no book. And so, in 1958, after four years of therapy, Connie simply withheld the sodium pentothal that Shirley was addicted to. Shirley was devastated. She wrote a long letter to Connie, admitting she was "none of the things I have pretended to be . . . I do not have any multiple personalities . . . I do not even have a 'double.'. . . I am all of them. I have been essentially lying."

Connie had a choice. She could give up the most important case of her career, or she could justify her misdiagnosis and failure to help her patient in familiar psychoanalytic jargon. Shirley, she explained, was experiencing massive denial and resistance—evidence that the therapy was working. Now Shirley had a choice. She could continue being a "multiple" and keep Connie and drugs in her life, or leave therapy, owing Connie a fortune she could never repay. Shirley went home and wrote Connie a second letter. It must have been another alter, she said, who wrote the first one. Connie upped Shirley's sessions to five a week and resumed the sodium pentothal.

In 1965, almost 11 years after their first psychotherapy session, Connie announced that she was moving to a new job in West Virginia. She told Shirley that she was welcome to come along, but she would have to integrate her multiple personalities right away so that the book could finally be written. Shirley immediately produced a new identity as herself and never again dissociated.

Flora faced her own choice about Sybil after finally getting a contract from a small publisher in 1969. Doing some investigative legwork for the book, she discovered huge discrepancies between Shirley's memories and what Shirley herself had written in her diaries at the time the alleged events occurred. If her mother went on lesbian orgies in the woods and defecated on neighbors' lawns, the young Shirley didn't say a word about it. No one in Shirley's hometown corroborated Shirley's memories, nor did her childhood medical records. And then Flora found Shirley's letter saying that she never had multiple personalities. Flora had to decide whether to give up this luscious project, which she was already fantasizing might be as successful as Truman Capote's *In Cold Blood*, or to believe Connie and Shirley.

When Ms. Nathan, as part of her own investigation, persuaded forensic experts to examine some of Shirley's key diaries, she learned that entries marked "1941" were written in ballpoint pen, which was not used in the United States until 1945. Ms. Nathan suspects Shirley wrote these entries years later, probably at Connie's urging, to support the MPD story and persuade Flora to stay with the project.

The Result of Suggestion

What, then, did Sybil suffer from? Is MPD "real"? Yes and no. MPD is what some psychiatrists call a culture-bound syndrome, a culturally permitted expression of extreme psychological distress, similar to an *ataque de nervios* (an episode of screaming, crying and agitation) in Hispanic cultures and "running amok" in Malaysia. As Ms. Nathan suggests, "the Sybil craze erupted during a fractured moment in history, when women pushed to go forward, even as the culture pulled back in fear."

The disorder seems real to clinicians and their patients who believe in it, but it results from suggestion, sometimes bordering on intimidation, by clinicians. One eminent MPD proponent actually told his colleagues that they might need to interview a patient for up to eight hours nonstop before an alter appears! Once that happens, the therapist rewards the patient with attention and praise for revealing more and more personalities, as Connie did to Sybil.

Flora Rheta Schreiber died in 1988, age 72. Her papers, including Sybil's therapy records, went to John Jay College in New York City, where they were sealed from public view to protect Sybil's identity. A decade later,

Psychiatrists' Views Toward the Diagnosis of Dissociative Identity Disorder

A total of 301 American psychiatrists were asked whether they thought dissociative amnesia and dissociative identity disorder (DID) should be included in the official listing of mental disorders, the DSM-IV, and whether there is strong scientific evidence that these disorders exist. Less than a quarter of them thought the evidence for the disorders is strong, and percent thought DID should be omitted from the list.

Question and Diagnosis	N	%	N	%	N	%	N	%
If DSM-IV were to be revised today, how should it treat the diagnosis of:	Should not be included at all		Should be included only with reservations		Should be included without reservations		No opinion	
Dissociative amnesia	27	9	143	48	104	35	27	9
Dissociative identity disorder	45	15	128	43	106	35	22	7
In your opinion, what is the status of scientific evidence regarding the validity of:	Little or no evidence of validity		Partial evidence of validity		Strong evidence of validity		No opinion	
Dissociative amnesia	56	19	145	48	69	23	31	10
Dissociative identity disorder	59	20	153	51	62	21	27	9

Taken from: Harrison G. Pope et al. "Attitudes Toward DSM-IV Dissociative Disorders Diagnoses Among Board-Certified American Psychiatrists." *American Journal of Psychiatry*, February 1999. http://ajp.psychiatryonline.org/article.aspx?articleid=173282.

diligent investigators discovered her real name, was opened to the public.

elia Wilbur died in 1992, age 86, when MPD was ght of popularity with her colleagues. Her execu-mer patient, destroyed her papers.

Shirley Mason died in 1998, at age 75, alone with a framed photo of Connie and the doll collection she had kept with her since childhood. In exchange for a life in Connie's orbit, she gave up close friends, enjoyable work as an art teacher and an offer of marriage to a man she loved.

The MPD bubble burst in 1995, when several patients sued a St. Paul psychiatrist for malpractice, alleging that she had used punitive methods to induce their "multiple personalities." They were awarded millions of dollars, and the psychiatrist eventually lost her medical license. More malpractice suits followed; hospitals closed their inpatient MPD units; and the epidemic subsided. Psychological researchers went on to scientifically discredit virtually all the assumptions underlying MPD, such as the belief that trauma is commonly repressed and causes "dissociation" of personality. Harvard psychologist Richard McNally calls this notion "a piece of psychiatric folklore devoid of convincing empirical support."

Misdiagnosis

Yet the promulgators of MPD do not seem to have learned anything. They changed the label to "Dissociative Identity Disorder," but a skunk by any other name is still a skunk. The International Society for the Study of Trauma and Dissociation continues to give its Cornelia B. Wilbur Award "for outstanding clinical contributions to the treatment of dissociative disorders." When Ms. Nathan told the society's president, Kathy Steele, about "the extensive evidence of Connie's ignorance, arrogance, and ethical misconduct" that she had unearthed, that Sybil was "a performance based on fiction," Ms. Steele replied: "So what? I don't know what difference it makes."

What difference does a correct diagnosis make? At a professional meeting in 1989, in response to a question from the audience about how Sybil was doing, Connie announced casually that Shirley suffered from pernicious anemia, a disease that causes an inability to process vitamin B-12. Discovering that Connie knew this fact about her patient may be Ms. Nathan's greatest scoop, for symptoms of pernicious anemia include just about everything that plagued Shirley Mason throughout her life: fatigue, social withdrawal, anxiety, hallucinations, muscle pains, confusion about identity, distorted memories and changes in personality. No one in Connie's audience of psychiatrists, Ms. Nathan writes, took note.

Whatever the Nature of Dissociative Identity Disorder, It Is a Serious Mental Illness

Charles Raison

In the following viewpoint Charles Raison notes that unlike psychiatric diagnoses that are controversial only among the general public, dissociative identity disorder is the focus of heated debate within the mental health field. Psychiatrists whose view centers on biological factors say it does not exist or that it is the result of the way therapists train their patients to interpret their symptoms. Advocates for the diagnosis point out that the different personalities of the same person have different electroencephalogram tracings. So, the author contends, the truth probably lies somewhere between these positions. Certainly dissociation is real, says Raison, and people who frequently dissociate have holes in their memories. This does not mean that they actually have many distinct personalities; they simply think of their experiences as happening to different people. It may do harm for a psychotherapist to treat them as if the separate personalities were real, and although these people are seriously ill, no effective form of treatment exists.

Raison is a psychiatrist at Emory University Medical School in Atlanta.

SOURCE: Charles Raison, "Is Dissociative Identity Disorder Real?," CNN.com, February 23, 2010. Copyright © 2010 by CNN. All rights reserved. Reproduced by permission.

Lots of psychiatric diagnoses generate controversy in the general public (e.g. attention deficit hyperactivity disorder, juvenile bipolar disorder), although they are noncontroversial in the mental health world. On the other hand, if you want to see mental health professionals spat with each other, ask a few of them what they think about dissociative identity disorder, the condition that used to be more colorfully known as multiple personality disorder.

Many biological psychiatrists who base their practices around medication management will tell you the condition doesn't exist, or that if it exists it is "iatrogenic," meaning it is caused by therapists training their patients to interpret their symptoms as if they have a whole set of distinct personalities. On the other hand, there are clinicians who specialize in the condition and they take the presence of multiple personalities so seriously that they will separate therapeutic meetings with each of a patient's "alters" (i.e. individual personalities). True believers will point to data that different personalities have different electroencephalogram tracings. Cynics will point out that actors can generate different EEG tracings when they switch characters.

As [do] all psychiatrists, I have my opinion about dissociative disorders. I like to think it is a middle-of-the-road position, but I'll let you judge for yourself.

The dictionary defines dissociation as "an unexpected partial or complete disruption of the normal integration of a person's conscious or psychological functioning that cannot be easily explained by the person." I don't think anyone could doubt that this phenomenon exists. You can do the mental experiment. Think about a time when you were driving a car and suddenly realized you'd completely lost attention to the last number of miles, or that you'd missed a turn without even realizing it. That is dissociation—you are doing something important and you lose track of the part of yourself that is doing it.

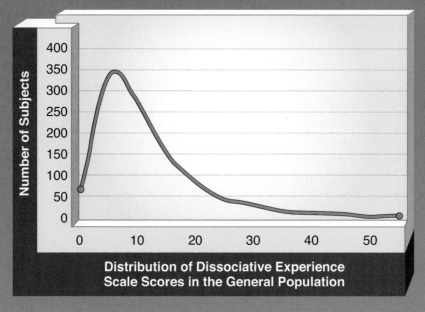

Percentage of People in One City Who Have Had Dissociative Experiences

In Winnipeg, Manitoba, Canada, 1,055 people in Winnipeg, Canada, filled out a questionnaire indicating how often they had had dissociative experiences (including normal dissociative experiences). Most of them had had very few. This questionnaire is used for screening, not diagnosis. The higher a person's score, the more likely it is that he or she *might* have a dissociative disorder.

Distribution of Dissociative Experience Scale Scores in the General Population

Number of Subjects

Taken from: "Dissociative Experiences Scale," Colin A. Ross Institute. http://rossinst.com/dissociative_experiences_scale.html.

Like all other mental difficulties, dissociation runs a spectrum from normal to extremely pathological. In my clinical experience it is very common for traumatized and/or very mentally ill people to manifest high rates of dissociation. People who dissociate a lot have conscious experience that is like Swiss cheese: full of holes. But unlike sadness, anger or clear psychosis, it is not usually readily apparent, so it gets less attention than it should. People who suffer with this rarely complain about it, because almost by definition, their fragmented conscious awareness makes it very difficult for them to even notice that they are missing things and/or not aware. We also do not have good pharmacological interventions to reduce dissociation, so it has gotten less money behind it than have many other mental conditions.

There is no doubt that some people behave as if they have multiple personalities. And not all of them have been to therapists who have trained them to interpret their dissociative experiences in this way. Does this mean that dissociative identity disorder exists? In my opinion it depends on what we mean by "exists." Yes, dissociative identity disorder exists if by *exists* we mean there are people who complain of its symptoms and suffer its consequences. Do I think that some people have many biologically distinct entities packed into their heads? No. I think that some people dissociate so badly that either on their own or as a result of therapeutic experiences it becomes the case that the most convincing way for them to see their own experience is as if it is happening to multiple people.

If this sounds like an endorsement of the condition, it is in a qualified way. I am personally less sanguine, however, about treatments that proceed as if each of the separate personalities really exists concretely and then work to integrate them again. This is the most common therapeutic way to treat the disorder, but I have seen precious few successes and a lot of people made worse by this intervention. In all fairness, however, I used to work intensively on inpatient psychiatric wards and had to care for the train wrecks left behind when integrative therapies failed, so maybe I'm negatively biased.

Here is a final strange paradox regarding the question of whether dissociative identity disorder exists. Whether clinicians believe or disbelieve, they will all tell you that

> ## FAST FACT
>
> Although dissociative identity disorder is diagnosed far more frequently in North America than in the rest of the world, a 1996 study found cases are found in other regions such as Turkey, leading researchers to believe that the disorder is not merely cultural.

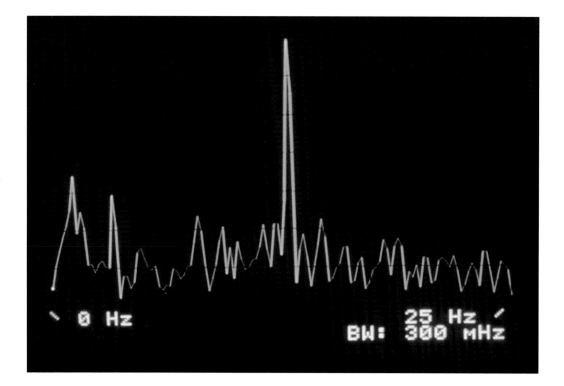

An electroencephalogram (EEG) shows brain activity. The different personalities of a person with DID can show different EEG tracings. (© Hank Morgan/Photo Researchers, Inc.)

it is one of the most serious psychiatric difficulties. Patients who demonstrate dissociative identity disorder symptoms are all extremely ill in my experience. They have frequently undergone significant trauma, especially early in life. The chaos of their personalities and behavior often leave a tornado track in their wake, and they suffer tremendous emotional discomfort and anxiety. And, as I mentioned above, unlike mental conditions such as depression or psychosis, for which good—although far from perfect—treatments exist, there is very little evidence that any currently available interventions are of much help.

People Who Function Well with Multiple Personalities Should Not Be Considered Ill

Anthony Temple

In the following viewpoint Anthony Temple argues that having multiple personalities is normal for some people and should not be viewed as illness unless it causes significant distress or impaired functioning. In some cultures it is considered an aspect of spirituality. Yet, he notes, in Western culture all portrayals of it are negative and therefore insulting to "multiples" who are happy with their condition and were not abused as children. Just as in the past when homosexuality was listed as an illness, says Temple, alleged experts are denying "different" people permission to exist. Temple asserts that dissociative identity disorder should not have been included in the diagnostic manual for psychiatrists, and its definition in the forthcoming new edition should be modified.

Temple is a multiple who functions well and has no desire to change. He writes extensively about issues concerning multiple personalitities at the website Astrea's Web.

SOURCE: Anthony Temple, "Multiplicity Is Natural," and "Removing Diagnostic Labels," Astraea's Web, June 17, 2011. Reproduced by permission.

Multiplicity is portrayed in the modern medical literature as invariably a dissociative disorder— a highly intelligent creative coping mechanism for dealing with childhoood trauma. This view is simplistic, disempowering, patronizing, and downright insulting to multiples who do not fit this limited profile. It implies that multiplicity is damage; that it is intrinsically wrong; that being single is normal and multiplicity is abnormal.

Multiplicity is a way of perceiving and relating to the world. The most current psychological research shows that it runs in families. The common thread in these families is not abuse, but creativity.

Considering what we know about the place of multiplicity in Southeast Asian, African and Afro-Cuban culture, I have focused on the fact that Western society has no template, no frame of reference, for non-pathological multiplicity. At least in the aforementioned societies, plurality is contextualized within the framework of spirituality. Multiplicity is viewed by African people from many nations, particularly the Yoruba, as "the spirits of your dead ancestors who give you advice or a push in the right direction".

This is of course not entirely a satisfactory reference point. Relegating it to the spiritual world puts it in the twilight realms—not necessarily altogether ooky, but certainly mysterious and spooky. Even in societies where belief in the spirit world is a part of routine, everyday life, there is still a frisson of fear, of worry that all is not as it should be, that it's *not normal.*

Still, at least it grants limited cultural permission. Children who show signs of being multiple are considered spiritual people, and are not killed to protect the community from evil (as multiple *births* often are). In certain native American tribes of the Gulf Coast regions, chiefs and spiritual leaders are chosen from among "those who have the most spirits living inside them." They may use meditation as a way of establishing intra-communication, but also possibly to make contact with an unseen world.

Distorted Views of Multiplicity

Western society has no such frame of reference, other than the mythology promulgated by the medical and media communities. Further, the inaccuracies in most public depictions are likely to generate more negative comparisons than positive ones. The one exception was [the TV series] *Herman's Head,* which was mostly wasted in conventional (albeit witty) sitcom absurdities.

Otherwise, *every* media portrayal of multiplicity has been stereotyped toward either helpless victims (women with glassy-eyed stares talking in a babylike lisp) or violent psychopaths (men with glassy-eyed stares flatly reciting the awful things George did). If I were multiple and didn't know it, and I were to see something like that on television, I would be much more likely to respond with "I'm NOT like that, so I can't possibly be multiple". Some of the groups who have appeared on talk shows have mentioned more common multiple experiences. *Not* the Dissociative Disorders Experience Scale which measures forgetfulness, but experiences of multiplicity—talk to myself, feel someone else is present, know that a given action or thought is not mine, etc. [Talk show host] Geraldo [Rivera] once presented a short list of these; but it's very difficult to explore them in the time allowed, when the majority of attention is focused on the morbidly sensational.

Western cultural and religious conditioning agree through implication that one body may contain one and only one person. Calling this assumption into question will force society to respond with all the defenses at its disposal (e.g. religious dogma, psychological theory, legalese, common sense, etc.).

I'm often asked why multiples invariably present with a history of childhood trauma. The answer may be more

> **FAST FACT**
>
> According to its website, the Icarus Project is one of many groups advocating for "a new culture and language that resonates" with actual experiences of those who are labeled "mentally ill." Members of this group believe these experiences are gifts and should not be labeled as disorders.

complex than Cornelia Wilbur [the psychiatrist who treated famed multiple "Sybil"] (and [founder of psychoanalysis Sigmund] Freud) would have liked us to believe.

The concept of multiplicity is so alien to some people that they need to find a way to fit it into their own worldview; writing it off by saying "Oh, those are people who were frightfully abused, it's quite unusual", is a convenient way to push both multiplicity and child abuse under the rug. In the process, they ignore an important reality. Child abuse is not rare. Physical and emotional abuse are intrinsic parts of Western culture. . . .

Not All Multiples Were Abused

So, some of the people who present at the doctor's office with issues stemming from child abuse, turn out to be multiple. In fact, they are *the only multiples to be registered, recognized, diagnosed*, in short, *the only multiples who are given cultural permission to exist!* Can we say "biased sampling?"

Any life situation, including childhood abuse, must affect the development of the persons in the [multiple] group, along with their operating system, that is, their style of management. Some people in the group may decide that it's their job to deal with certain aspects of the abuse, perhaps that they were born for that purpose. Or they may feel that they exist independently and just need to deal with what is happening.

I think this may be one of the origins of the sort of operating system you read about in the popular literature; a frontrunner who doesn't know she's multiple, while the rest of the people run things smoothly from behind the scenes. As life situations change, an operating system might need to be tweaked, updated, or scrapped completely for a new one. The frontrunner becomes aware of the others, fears insanity, presents for therapy, and things proceed a la Truddi Chase [the author of an autobiography about being a multiple]. This, of course, is not the scenario for every multiple who's experienced abuse, or even for every situation in which a single frontrunner is kept in the dark.

I also don't believe that every multiple in the above situation was necessarily traumatized or abused in the conventional sense. Because there is no model for multiplicity in this society other than the ghastly portrayals in tabloid TV and horror movies, multiples who don't fit this pattern are, in effect, *non-persons*. They literally do not exist according to the current mode of western thought. There is no cultural permission for them to exist. The mental health industry confirms this by labeling multiplicity as a disorder. The courts confirm it every time a multiple in trouble with the law gets a NGRI [not guilty by reason of insanity] verdict. So, a frontrunner or two may not realize they are part of a strong, smoothly functional multiple system because they have never been informed that such a thing can exist.

In some cultures, children that show signs of DID are considered spiritual people and treated as special. (© Bryan and Cherry Alexander/Photo Researchers, Inc.)

Back to abuse for a minute: Chris Costner-Sizemore (the woman whose life story was the basis for movie *The Three Faces of Eve*) showed us that a multiple can be abused *because they are multiple*. Children in multiple systems may have certain experiences and may behave in ways which irritate authority figures. Lack of consciousness between persons in the group is a common source of said irritant. So is "I didn't do it, Bobby did it." Supposedly there is research being done into recognizing childhood multiplicity, but it's all preventative, eradicatory stuff. Nothing is being done simply to help children within a group who may be having a little trouble working out their own functional operating systems.

There is no model for non-pathological multiplicity in Western society. In fact, there is barely a model for multiplicity at all. Singlet "experts" like [psychiatrist] Colin Ross are doing their damnedest to make sure that there never will be. The situation is redolent of the 1960s headline, "Homosexuality: Sin or Sickness?" . . .

Removing Diagnostic Labels

Possibly one of the worst things that ever happened to multiples was when the American Psychological Association declared multiplicity an official "mental disorder" worthy of inclusion in the *Diagnostic and Statistical Manual* [DSM].

Although this may have been beneficial to numerous people who genuinely needed help with disorganised systems and hadn't been able to get any, it also named the condition of being multiple, in and of itself, as a mental disease.

This was done partly at the behest of well-meaning feminists, the Religious Right, and child-welfare crusaders who honestly believed Connie Wilbur's ludicrous theory that multiplicity was always a form of dissociative mental illness caused by severe, often sexual, child abuse. They were justifiably anxious to do something to stop child abuse and help those suffering from its aftereffects years later.

What might have made more sense in retrospect is to expand the category of delayed stress or post-traumatic stress disorder to include the unique difficulties suffered by adults and children who have been abused, and leave multiplicity out of it. Or better yet, to create a separate category for multiples who *are* in disarray and need help organising things.

Instead, multiples, singlets, and abuse survivors fell prey to overzealous crusaders like Elizabeth Humenansky, cultmeisters like Bennet Braun and Colin Ross, and the despicable False Memory Syndrome Foundation. Sincere doctors suffered as well. Those who made attempts at genuine help for disordered households, or any kind of serious study of multiplicity, have now fallen into disfavour. Thanks to right-wing ideologues like psychiatrist Paul McHugh, it is modish to dismiss multiplicity as an hysterical media-generated fantasy, and the label's been changed from "MPD" to "DID" [multiple personality disorder to dissociative identity disorder], to appease the white singlet males who run the psychiatric industry. Now, multiple households who need or want treatment have a harder time than ever trying to get it.

Labeling Only Dysfunctional Multiples

I've heard the argument that the diagnostic label was supposed to ensure that multiples who needed therapy could get it, and for their insurance to cover the cost of treatment. I get many more emails from multiples who, even during the heyday of the MPD/recovery movement, were told "there is no such thing", "no real multiple knows that she is or will admit it if she knows", and at least one who reported his therapist was fired merely for giving him a DID diagnosis.

Since the DSM-IV is also a legal reference guide for state of mind in criminal cases, one would think

Sample Statements from a Dissociative Identity Disorder Diagnostic Test

Teens are asked to say whether these statements describe them in a diagnostic test for dissociative identity disorder, known as the Adolescent Dissociative Experience Scale (A-DES) . The comments are by Dr. Numan Gharaibeh, a psychiatrist who does not believe that the test is valid.

A-DES: *I get so wrapped up in watching TV, reading, or playing a video game that I don't have any idea what's going on around me.*

Comment: Although this item seems like a joke, it is not meant as one. It is meant to be part of the serious business of science. Isn't that what any "normal" human would do if he or she has enough attention and concentration?

A-DES: *People tell me I do or say things that I don't remember doing or saying.*

I get confused about whether I have done something or only thought about doing it.

I can't figure out if things really happened or if I only dreamed or thought about them.

People tell me that I sometimes act so differently that I seem like a different person.

Comment: These items are crafted in a way to encourage false positives. First, "people tell me" does not qualify as an "experience." Second, one wonders why the scale was made up of declarative statements instead of questions. Third, "I seem like a different person" is a leading statement.

A-DES: *I am so good at lying and acting that I believe it myself.*

Comment: This should be an immediate tip-off that the reporter is unreliable.

A-DES: *I feel like my past is a puzzle and some pieces are missing.*

Comment: Isn't this the human condition?

Taken from: Numan Gharaibeh. "Dissociative Identity Disorder: Time to Remove It from DSM-V?" *Current Psychiatry*, September 2009. www.ptsdforum.org/c/gallery/-pdf/1-39.pdf.

that including multiple personality in the DSM was a good way to protect multiple systems in which one or more members have run afoul of the law. Generally, a multiple-personality defense is indistinguishable from the standard Not Guilty By Reason of Insanity plea. Multiplicity is not insanity, and it should *not* be a legal defense for criminal behaviour. Members of multiple households need to be organized enough to create a working system that ensures responsible behaviour. Realistically, there will always be systems in chaos who could benefit from a course in household management. What would make much more sense is to create a category, specifically, of *disordered multiples,* not simply to define all multiples as disordered.

When homosexuality was deleted from the Big Red Book [the DSM] after the industry finally accepted the reality that it's not a mental disease, it was replaced with "ego-dystonic homosexuality", so that the few gay people who did view it as a disorder could still receive help. I suggest something similar for multiplicity, to be taken seriously and not as a "junk" diagnosis. In this way, multiples who see themselves as conforming to the Wilburian pattern and who may wish to be integrated, can seek appropriate services; and systems in chaos whose out-of-control selves commit serious crimes can receive treatment that will benefit the group, and ultimately, society-at-large. . . .

Proposed Change to the DSM

The fifth edition—DSM-5—is now being put together by teams of specialists. . . . There is a crucial change being proposed in the diagnostic criteria for "dissociative identity disorder", and public comment is invited.

This is what "dissociative identity disorder" will look like in the DSM-5 if the proposed changes are accepted.

A. Disruption of identity characterized by two or more distinct personality states or an experience of possession, as evidenced by discontinuities in sense of self, cognition, behavior, affect, perceptions, and/or memories. This disruption may be observed by others or reported by the patient.

B. Inability to recall important personal information, for everyday events or traumatic events, that is inconsistent with ordinary forgetfulness.

C. Causes clinically significant distress or impairment in social, occupational, or other important areas of functioning.

[In other words, if this criterion is included, if being multiple does not interfere with your everyday life then you do not have Dissociative Identity Disorder.]

D. The disturbance is not a normal part of a broadly accepted cultural or religious practice and is not due to the direct physiological effects of a substance (e.g., blackouts or chaotic behavior during Alcohol intoxication) or a general medical condition (e.g., complex partial seizures). NOTE: In children, the symptoms are not attributable to imaginary playmates or other fantasy play.

Specify if:

a) With non-epileptic seizures or other conversion symptoms

b) With somatic symptoms that vary across identities (excluding those in specifier a)

Criterion C is intended to distinguish DID from culturally accepted multiplicity. If this criterion is included, natural and self-recognized multiples can be out in therapy without necessarily getting a DID diagnosis.

It may help group members who seek professional help with issues unrelated to being multiple. There will be more of a chance that group members can help provide background information or insights without fear of being classified as mere symptoms of a mental disease.

Of course, it will take decades before professionals really accept that non-disordered multiplicity is possible, but this is an important step.

Experts Disagree About Whether Dissociative Amnesia Can Occur After Child Abuse

Robert J. Cordy

The following court opinion describes the testimony given at the trial of Paul Shanley, a former priest accused of having sexually abused a boy who did not remember the incidents until twenty years after they occurred. The case received wide media attention. Prominent psychiatrists were called as expert witnesses to testify as to whether the victim's testimony concerning his recovered memories was credible. The expert for the prosecution said that dissociative amnesia is a recognized diagnosis, that it is not rare, and that an emotional trigger can cause repressed memories of abuse to be recovered. The witness for the defense said her research has shown that eyewitness testimony is not always reliable, that people can be implanted with entirely false memories, and that there is no way to tell true memories from false ones.

Robert J. Cordy, a justice of the Supreme Judicial Court of Massachusetts, wrote this opinion denying the petition of the defendant for a new trial.

SOURCE: Robert J. Cordy, "Court's Opinion, *Commonwealth v. Shanley*," Supreme Judicial Court of Massachusetts, January 15, 2010.

The Commonwealth called Dr. James A. Chu as an expert in the field of dissociative amnesia [during Paul Shanley's trial for child sexual abuse]. He was not called to give a diagnosis of the victim, but rather to assist the jury in determining the credibility of the victim's testimony that he had recovered memories nearly twenty years after the abuse, and their consequent reliability. His qualifications as an expert were not contested by the defendant at trial.

Dr. Chu testified that dissociative amnesia is a diagnosis included and defined in the *Diagnostic and Statistical Manual* (DSM). That manual is published by the American Psychiatric Association, and is a classification manual widely used by mental health professionals in making diagnoses of mental health problems. The DSM lists criteria for a clinician to consider when making a particular diagnosis. Dr. Chu was a member of the task force in the 1990's charged with reviewing dissociative disorder diagnoses for the purpose of preparing the most recent version of the DSM, DSM-IV, which was published in 1994. He explained that in the DSM-IV, dissociative amnesia is a "descriptive term [for] somebody who cannot remember certain important information about themselves, either about what happened to them, sometimes personal information . . . not . . . due to . . . head trauma or intoxication." It means, "basically, that there is a dissociative barrier that prevents somebody from remembering something in their ordinary state of consciousness."

Recovered Memories

In describing how dissociative amnesia works, Dr. Chu testified that it is possible for a person to forget something and remember it later. Dr. Chu observed the phenomenon in his own clinical practice with adults who had been traumatized as children and explained that while it was not common in that population, it was "not at all rare." He analogized dissociative amnesia to a type of forgetting, which "leads to people having really pervasive amnesia for not only [traumatic] events themselves, but [also] sometimes for neutral events or even good events." He explained that persons who have experienced repeated traumatization suffer from dissociative amnesia more often than those who experience a single traumatic event.

He went on to testify that when a person remembers "so-called forgotten memories," it is usually the result of a "trigger of some kind" which reminds that person of the traumatic experience. While there was no typical pattern for the subsequent reaction of a traumatized person once there has been a trigger, the person may experience memory flashes or "body sensations." More specifically, a person might experience physical sensations that mirror the sensations he or she incurred from the trauma itself (for example, genital pain where a person had suffered sexual abuse); or have a subsequent reaction to a trigger, become overwhelmed by the sudden onset of traumatic memories and experience "people panic," that is, agitation, crying, and increased adrenaline. He further explained that, although it is "highly variable" among individuals, the return of such memories may lead to disruption or dysfunction in a person's life.

Dr. Chu also testified about the quality of the memory that might be recovered with the caveat that "all . . . memories are subject to various kinds of distortion." In general, however, "the central themes of memories are really relatively well-preserved," with distortions as to peripheral details and perhaps the sequence of the memory. He also explained that a person may not remember everything about a particular event all at once, that instead, the memory might progressively return. Dr. Chu identified the ways in which a clinician would go about testing the validity of a memory recovered many years later, including determining whether a person's life changed abruptly at a certain time, whether the person has had the ability to begin and maintain interpersonal relationships, and whether the narrative of the person's life is believable and reasonable.

Dr. Chu acknowledged that it was possible for a new memory to be created in some people that has no basis in reality. He gave common examples of this phenomenon on a minor scale, but explained that there was "probably only a very small minority of people who are vulnerable to that kind of suggestion."

Dr. Chu concluded by estimating that dissociative amnesia occurs in approximately twenty per cent of the seriously traumatized population.

The Defense's Case

The defense at trial was threefold: first, that the abuse did not happen; second, that the victim had significant financial and personal reasons to fabricate the abuse; and third, that the theory of repressed memory is inherently unreliable given the problem with corroboration and the possibility of false memories. The first two prongs of the defense were presented through the cross-examination of the Commonwealth's witnesses. The third was developed initially through the cross-examination of Dr. Chu, during which he acknowledged that there are professionals in the psychiatric community who do not believe there is sufficient evidence to verify the existence of dissociative amnesia, and that clinical research on the subject relies to a significant extent on the self-reporting of the patient—a methodological limitation. This prong of the defense was enhanced by the testimony of Dr. Elizabeth Loftus, an expert witness, and the only witness called by the defense.

Dr. Loftus is a professor at the University of California at Irvine in the Department of Psychology and Social Behavior and the Department of Criminology, Law, and Society. She is also a member and former president of the American Psychological Society, which has several thousand members focusing on the science and teaching sides of psychology. Her qualifications as an expert were not contested by the Commonwealth at trial.

Dr. Loftus testified that she has conducted research on memory and memory distortion, including experiments in the 1970's and 1980's where her research group evaluated the reliability of eyewitness testimony to a simulated accident or crime scene by subjecting the eyewitnesses to misinformation, such as leading questions or media accounts of the incident, to determine the impact, if any, on their recall of the event. She further elaborated that her research in the 1990's expanded the theories of misinformation to see whether people could be implanted with entirely false memories, for example, by making a person think that he or she had been lost in a shopping mall as a child. She explained that one quarter of the persons involved in this experiment believed in the false memory of being lost.

False Memories

Dr. Loftus described memory as involving the construction or reconstruction of experiences where a person may blend later occurring details into the memory of an event. She explained that many things could affect the accuracy of a memory, including factors related to the perception of an event as it occurs, such as lighting and distance and the exposure to postevent information such as leading questions or media coverage, which can distort or supplement a memory. Dr. Loftus also explained that the passage of time made memories weaker and thus more vulnerable to postevent contamination. She explained that a false memory is a false belief accompanied by sensory detail.

In addition, Dr. Loftus testified that it was "virtually impossible without independent corroboration" to determine the difference between an accurate memory and a false one. She stated that the impact of trauma on a memory is that

> **FAST FACT**
>
> During the past few decades there have been many lawsuits and/or criminal charges brought by adults against their parents or others they came to believe had abused them in childhood, and some against therapists accused of having produced false memories of childhood abuse in their clients.

while the core of the memory might be recalled, the peripheral details may be distorted. In contrast to Dr. Chu, Dr. Loftus testified that repetitive traumatic experience would make it more likely that someone would remember a particular event.

She elaborated on the controversy surrounding "repressed memory" and explained that in her view of the literature there is no "credible scientific evidence for the idea that years of brutalization can be massively repressed." She noted that it was possible to retrieve unpleasant memories through ordinary remembering and forgetting, but there was a lack of current scientific support for the theory that some "special mechanism" would "banish [traumatic experience] into the unconscious." She also explained that there was "inherent limitation" in the method of studies used to test for repressed memory, namely, that the retrospective memory technique relies on self-reporting by patients. . . .

In this case, the victim was expected to testify that he had been abused many years ago, but had only recently remembered that abuse. To assist the jury in understanding how memories of abuse might be forgotten and later remembered, the Commonwealth proposed to offer expert witness testimony to explain the theory, condition, and symptoms of dissociative amnesia and recovered memory. In response, the defendant moved to preclude such testimony because the theory underlying it could not meet the test of reliability required for admission. . . .

Further Testimony

Despite his misgivings about whether it was required, the judge [of the lower court] proceeded to conduct a Lanigan hearing [a hearing to determine whether an expert witness's testimony is scientifically reliable] that extended over five days. During that hearing, two experts retained by the Commonwealth, Dr. Daniel Brown and Dr. Chu, were called to testify. In addition to this testi-

Dr. James A. Chu, an expert in dissociative amnesia, has testified that it is possible for a person to repress a memory and then remember it later. (© AP Images/Chitose Suzuki)

mony, the judge considered, without objection from the Commonwealth, an affidavit prepared by Dr. Loftus and submitted by the defendant.

Dr. Brown was called by the Commonwealth to explain the theory, conditions, and symptoms of dissociative amnesia and recovered memory and their general acceptance in the scientific community. Dr. Chu, who had been retained by the Commonwealth, was called to testify about the "fit" of the proposed opinion testimony regarding dissociative amnesia and recovered memory, to the facts of this case. . . .

Dr. Brown testified that based on his clinical experience, his review of thousands of studies regarding various aspects of memory, and his analysis of eighty-five studies focused on amnesia in childhood sexual abuse cases, many of which were subject to peer review, it was his opinion that dissociative amnesia exists for a clinically significant minority of traumatized individuals, including children subjected to sexual abuse. He also testified about the evolution of the use of dissociative amnesia as a diagnosis in the DSM, which has been revised several times. He opined that this diagnosis is generally accepted in the field and cited six surveys of psychology professionals, including psychiatrists, psychologists, social workers and clinicians working with war veterans, to that effect. According to those surveys (taken collectively), eighty-nine per cent of those surveyed accepted the validity or possible validity of dissociative amnesia.

Dr. Brown acknowledged that there is controversy surrounding the existence of dissociative amnesia and the difficulty in determining its existence in a particular individual. He also highlighted some of the problems with determining the existence of dissociative amnesia, and agreed that a person with a suggestible personality might be susceptible to false memories suggested by a trusted source, and that an extremely suggestive process of interviewing a subject could also create false memories.

Defense counsel cross-examined Dr. Brown for two days about the problems affiliated with determining the existence of repressed memory; the difficulties of corroborating the details of recovered memories; the difficulty in making a precise diagnosis in accordance with the DSM-IV; the uncertainty as to the cause or neurological or biological mechanisms that lead to dissociative amnesia; and the likelihood that a particularly suggestible person would develop false memories or malinger. In that examination, defense counsel brought to the judge's attention the contentions of the critics of repressed memory theory based on the lack of a scientific method to test for it in individuals; the absence of a controlled methodology; and the methodological limitations of clinical observation and experience that depend so greatly on patient self-reporting.

The Judge's Decision

The judge denied the defendant's motion to exclude expert testimony on dissociative amnesia and recovered memory, concluding that the diagnosis and theories behind it were generally accepted in the relevant scientific community. In doing so, the judge recognized the significance of its listing as a diagnosis in DSM-IV, and credited the testimony of Dr. Brown that "clinically significant minorities of [victims of child sexual abuse] experience amnesia," testimony that was buttressed by the studies cited to and relied on by Dr. Brown which "reflect[ed] a broad-based acceptance of dissociative amnesia and recovery." Contrary to the defendant's arguments that controversy regarding the validity of a theory necessarily precluded a determination that the theory is generally accepted, the judge recognized the controversy, was fully aware of its contours, and rejected it as being determinative in light of the other evidence of acceptance. That other evidence, the judge pointed out, included statements of both the American Medical Association and the American [Psychiatric] Association, that "memories of traumatic events can be forgotten but that pseudomemory formation is also possible," in addition to the 1996 final report of the American Psychological Association working group on the investigation of memories of childhood abuse, which included points of agreement among the group members (including Dr. Loftus) that (1) it is possible for memories of abuse that have been forgotten for a long time to be remembered, and (2) it is also possible to construct convincing pseudo memories for events that never occurred. . . .

The judge, while well apprised of the contention that studies of dissociative amnesia are unreliable because of methodological flaws, explicitly found that "the methodological criticisms . . . by Dr. Loftus [in her affidavit were] rebutted [by Dr. Brown in his testimony]."

In sum, the judge's finding that the lack of scientific testing did not make unreliable the theory that an individual may experience dissociative amnesia was supported in the record, not only by expert testimony but by a wide collection of clinical observations and a survey of academic literature.

The Definitions of the Dissociative Disorders May Soon Be Changed

Paul

Psychiatrists are currently revising the *Diagnostic and Statistical Manual of Mental Disorders,* which is used to define the criteria by which patients can be diagnosed. The author of the following viewpoint says the definitions of the dissociative disorders will probably be changed because there are many psychiatrists who do not agree with them. There may be a new heading that will include both post-traumatic stress disorder (PTSD) and dissociative disorders, which are widely believed to be the result of extreme stress. Or a new type of dissociative disorder may be added as a subtype of PTSD, since some forms of PTSD are characterized by dissociation. No definition of a disorder can be perfect, notes the author, but the new manual should aim for the best possible categorization of symptoms.

Paul is a scientist, educator, photographer, and musician. He is the owner of the blog *Mind Parts*, in which he comments on insights he has gained as a survivor of childhood sexual abuse.

In an editorial to the most recent *Journal of Trauma and Dissociation*, Dr. David Spiegel writes about how dissociation will likely be addressed in the forthcoming DSM5 [the 5th edition of the *Diagnostic and Statistical Manual of Mental Disorders*]. For those of you not familiar, the *Diagnostic and Statistical Manual of Mental Disorders*, commonly referred to as the DSM, is psychiatry's approach to standardizing mental disorders. I understand how many look askew at any psychiatric labels, myself sometimes included. But there is the reality that correct diagnoses are an important component to healing. Having a manual and common language helps to increase recognition, accurate assessment, and align treatments.

There has been some concern that the dissociative disorders, especially dissociative identity disorder, would be subsumed under other diagnoses and thereby essentially be "declassified." Even now, despite their presence in the current DSM, they are not well integrated into the psychiatric community. There are large biases against dissociation, that strangely do not seem to be as apparent in illnesses such as depression or schizophrenia. Probably this is due to the sometimes ephemeral nature of impairment. To the observer, it often appears that dissociatives can just pull themselves together, lending some credence to the belief that no real disorder exists. Yet, to the dissociative, we know there is much more to what we deal with than just being able to pull ourselves together. We know about what it means to lose our identity, to have huge gaps in memory, to have wild swings of consciousness. And, as I have said before, I believe one of the main reasons for the bias is that many clinicians and lay people are uncomfortable with the notion that an adult human being can have a fragmented sense of identity or lose control of their minds and bodies.

> **FAST FACT**
>
> Diagnostic labels for mental disorders are necessary not only because they provide mental health professionals with a common language, but because without a recognized diagnosis, medical insurance will not pay for the help a person may need.

Proposed Diagnostic Changes

In his editorial, Spiegel, a member of the DSM5 Task Force, asserts that the dissociative disorders will be included in the revision which will come out in 2013. He gave a summary of what the task force is proposing. They are proposing that there be a stress and trauma spectrum section which will include PTSD [post-traumatic stress disorder] and the dissociative disorders. In so doing, the DSM5 will [emphasize] the common etiology [origin] of these "disorders." This would be a controversial move, since the current version focuses more on description of symptoms. Even though there would still not be a diagnostic requirement of a trauma for a dissociative disorder to exist, placing dissociation squarely into a section with an emphasis on trauma etiology would be a blow to the false memory advocates. It would be a validation and positive step for those of us who appreciate that dissociative disorders do have a strong basis in trauma.

In fact, it appears that this trauma etiology will be pursued even further based on studies by Ruth Lanius and colleagues that there is a substantial subgroup, of nearly one third, of those with post-traumatic stress disorder showing mainly symptoms of dissociation which are far different from the "classic" PTSD symptoms. These clinical findings are supported by the functional MRI [magnetic resonance imaging] studies which show that the dissociative subgroup has increased prefrontal cortical activity and reduced limbic activity in response to traumatic stimuli, which is *opposite* of the typical PTSD response.

One of the proposed changes to the criteria for dissociative identity disorder I think is a step back. It states that the disruption of identity "may be observed by others, or reported by the patient." Detractors of dissociative identity disorder will say that there is no clinical input. On the other hand, there are clearly disorders where there is primarily patient reporting. Depression comes to mind. The onus would then be on the clinician to deter-

mine whether the self-reporting of the patient is consistent with the rest of the criteria for the disorder to warrant the diagnosis.

Complex PTSD, as proposed by Judith Herman in 1992, is not addressed in the current DSM and appears not to be addressed in the DSM5. I think this is for good reason. To do so, would confound matters. The commonly understood symptoms of complex PTSD are basically PTSD symptoms plus overlap with many other areas (such as anxiety, personality, and dissociative disorders). I think we all, patients and clinicians alike, need to appreciate that the DSM will always have limitations. The manifestations of all of these disorders in practice are almost always more complex than any manual can ever hope to capture. But the goal of the manual should be to make a best effort and provide a guidepost.

The *Diagnostic and Statistical Manual of Mental Disorders*, being revised for 2013, may have a stress and trauma section that includes both post-traumatic stress disorder and dissociative disorders. (© AP Images/Mark Zdechlik)

CHAPTER 3

Personal Narratives

A College Student Describes What Dissociative Depersonalization Feels Like

TwentyHundredHeartbeats

The author began having depersonalization experiences when she was six years old. As a child she found them terrifying. When she was in the fifth grade she spent a whole summer feeling as if she were living in a dream. Her dissociative disorder caused even more anxiety when she entered high school. She thought she was going insane because she knew that such feelings are not normal, and when she tried to explain them to her boyfriend he did not understand. Believing that she was the only person who had ever felt that way, she became very depressed. The counselor she went to mistakenly thought that the depression was her only problem. Finally, in her senior year, she went to a psychologist who eventually diagnosed her condition accurately, and knowing that it has a name and that she is not alone makes it easier to cope with.

The author, whose blogging handle is TwentyHundredHeartbeats, was in college studying human services at the time of writing this viewpoint.

Photo on facing page. Former Olympian and pro football player Herschel Walker has written a book about his struggle with dissociative identity disorder. (© **Tom Lau/ Landov**)

My experience with depersonalization, and derealization as well, began when I was six years old. At that time of course, and up until the past couple of years, I didn't know that's what I was experiencing. Any kind or symptom of dissosication disorders can be *terrifying*, at any age, especially for young children. I remember having the feeling of what I described at the time of being "two different people". Not two different personalities, but having a complete detachment of who I was . . . when I placed a name in my head to who I was and where I lived, it was confusing and caused a great amount of anxiety for me. I had obsessive thoughts (particularly before I went to sleep) to remind myself of who I was, because I would spend days at a time disconnected from my reality, or from who I was. I was unfamiliar with my "being".

I know this is so hard and strange to explain, but I am hoping those of you who have experienced this, will understand.

Anyway, I experienced this feeling very often until about the fifth grade age, when I remember spending an *entire* summer in a "dream" like state. . . . Yes I was there doing my daily tasks and routines, but I would occasionally have this feeling of "waking up" or coming back to my full being, while at all other times I felt like I was dreaming! I felt like everything was surreal. I felt the motions and words said by the people around me were very mechanic and part of a dream. In addition, I felt myself drawing back and secluding myself because when I participated I was more likely to have to observe myself and have the dream feeling which caused a lot of anxiety. I was also very shy to talk to people about this sensation because it seemed impossible to explain. How do you explain that you constantly feel like you are not who you are, not that you don't "fit in", but that you literally feel completely mentally non-associated with your being besides a few moments where you are drawn back in, only to find you missed parts of hours, days, and even in that situation months of a summer. Not that I didn't remember what had happened, because my memory would be intact, but rather my emotional capabilities during the dream like state, and out of them, were drastically different.

When I entered high school, and the end of middle school, this dissociative disorder really caused a lot of anxiety for me. I was convinced I was insane. As far as I knew no normal person had the feeeling of "leaving" their body. I was sure I was crazy. I tried to explain to my high school boyfriend, who was my closest friend at the time, and although he sympathized he did not nearly understand or comprehend the extent of this experience. The amount of stress these feelings and disorder I was living with caused me, forced me into a deep depression. It was impossible to bear the thought of forever having these feelings and experiences without anyone ever being able to understand. Not to mention I truly believed I was the only one who experienced this!!

Seeking a Diagnosis

Early 9th grade year, I went to a counselor for the first time. I was completely embarrassed and reluctant to explain what was going on. She attributed my withdrawing from social situations and constant worry to depression.

As I grew older my dissociative disorder and anxiety (in general) became less frequent in my life. I learned to cope, but not well. I just had the tendency to push the feelings aside. They were stressful and I felt I was going to have them *forever*.

In my senior year of high school I was fed up. I had had multiple anxiety attacks, which in my own mind I attributed to depersonalization . . . they were confusing, stressful, and preoccupied my thoughts. I was in and out of depression and felt the person I was closest to was myself. I constantly felt different, paranoid, I wanted a

The author remembers one summer spent in a dreamlike state. She felt everything was surreal and that the people around her were just part of that dream. (© nagelestock.com/Alamy)

normal mind. I wanted healthy thoughts. I wanted the obsessive worries about being crazy to go away!

I met with a psychologist, who at first, like the last attributed my worries to Generalized Anxiety Disorder [GAD] as I continued to meet with her and eventually open up to her about the sensaton of being disconnected from myself in every sense, about out-of-body experience feelings. She began to truly see the extent of my suffering. Mental disorders weigh a toll on a persons confidence in themselves, even their sanity if they don't know otherwise. . . . She gave me a proper diagnosis of dissociative depersonalization/derealization disorder in combination with GAD.

Just having a diagnosis really can help to ease your worries. You are not alone, when you begin to have the symptoms of your disorder. . . . I am able to remind myself "there is a name for this, you are not crazy, it *will* go away, you *can* be open with people close to you about your experiences".

I am now in my junior year of college, studying human services. My depersonalization experiences are far less frequent as I am learning how to better manage my anxiety. Although it can still be a struggle, and the experiences still are *terrifying* i know that i am not "crazy" and that if I choose, I can explain this disorder to others close to me by educating myself about it.

I do attribute the onset of my dissociative disorder and my GAD to experiences in my childhood which I never knew how to tolerate, deal with, or express openly.

An Attorney Tells How She Learned to Deal with Dissociative Identity Disorder

Olga Trujillo

Olga Trujillo, a survivor of child abuse, felt as if her mind was a house with many rooms, some of which she could not unlock because they held unbearable memories. She had a central sense of self that kept those memories out of her consciousness by distracting her with anxiety and worry. Then, when she became an adult and the doors started to open, she was terrified and confused and lacked a normal sense of her body. Eventually, however, she was able to integrate the separate parts of herself and gain a sense of confidence.

Trujillo is an attorney, independent consultant, and nationally renowned speaker dedicated to combating violence against women and children. She is the author of *The Sum of My Parts: A Survivor's Story of Dissociative Identity Disorder.*

I was recently asked during a presentation on trauma and dissociation what having parts feels like on the inside.

It wasn't until I started healing and integrating that I understood how different it felt to be a person with a divided consciousness rather than a person with a whole sense of consciousness.

When my mind was divided it was organized like a house with many rooms. Some rooms were created to hold unbearable memories, to keep them away from my consciousness. Those doors were painted black and I was unable to find the key to unlock them. Other rooms, bright and colorful, I came and went from easily. All these rooms were created instinctively by my mind in response to the relentless abuse I suffered at the hands of my father and others while growing up.

I was lucky to have a central sense of self—like a stage director—who could collect and store information in the bright rooms. This central Me also locked the dark doors and kept their existence away from my consciousness. Any time something threatened to remind me of the information those doors hid, the central Me cleverly rushed in with anxiety, racing thoughts in English and Spanish, and obsessive worry. Anyone watching me would have thought me to be fidgety, distracted, talkative, nervous, and compulsive about tidying.

Opening Doors

As an adult, my life became much more stable and safe. With my greater capacity to handle the information the dark rooms contained, their doors began to open unexpectedly. The emotions and pain that came rushing from them were overwhelming. They felt like they would overtake me. I was flooded with the terror I had felt when I was attacked as a child. Even though the central Me knew I was bigger, stronger, and no longer in danger, I believed that I would die. I felt small and defenseless. My thoughts came in Spanish again, even though it had been years since I had spoken Spanish regularly. These were signs of the parts of my consciousness.

My body began to seem less defined. I didn't have a good sense of how big or small I was. The limits of where my body started and ended were fuzzy so I often had bruises from bumping into things. My hands felt too big for me at times. I looked in the mirror and was surprised at the person I saw. She seemed to be much older than me. My feet looked big, my legs long.

Once I started to integrate these separate aspects of myself, throwing open all those doors, I started to feel calmer. I had less thoughts running through my mind, interrupting my day. I slept better. I was less distracted and could concentrate better.

Olga likens her experience with dissociative identity disorder to being in a place with many locked doors. As she grew into adulthood the doors began to open. (© Brian Young/ Alamy)

Over time, I integrated more and more of the rooms in the house into the central part of me. I started becoming whole. I started breaking down the walls of each room, creating an open floor plan in my mind. As this happened, my sense of calm deepened and I gained a sense of confidence I had never felt before. I felt clearer and sharper in my mind and in my sense of my body. My hands looked like they belonged to me again. I looked like I thought I should when I looked in the mirror. I began to feel more capable and my emotions stabilized. A sense of confidence grew in me that I could ride out the terror, fear, anger and loss that those locked rooms held.

A Writer Describes His Experience with Depersonalization Disorder

Jeffrey Abugel

When Jeffrey Abugel was young he had a sudden experience of feeling shattered, as if attacked from without or within, and the fragments of himself returned only over time. It seemed to him as if he were observing himself and did not have normal human thoughts or feelings. He was sure no one else felt that way. But after eleven years with a terrifying sense of strangeness and unreality, when none of the many doctors he visited could say what was wrong with him, he finally found one who told him that his condition is called depersonalization disorder (DPD) and that it is very common.

Abugel is a writer and former editor of numerous *Better Homes and Gardens* magazines. He is the author of *Stranger to My Self*, from which this excerpt was taken, and coauthor of *Feeling Unreal: Depersonalization Disorder and the Loss of the Self*.

SOURCE: Jeffrey Abugel, "Introduction," *Stranger to My Self Insider Depersonalization: The Hidden Epidemic.* Carson, VA: Johns Road Publishing, 2010. pp. xi-xiii.

Some time long ago, when I was young and on the verge of adulthood, my soul departed.

It shot out suddenly, forcefully, spewing like pus from an acrid sore. Or, perhaps it was more an implosion that only killed within, forcing "me" further inward until, like a black hole, its destructive density annihilated its captive. Whether some thing attacked me from without, or within, doesn't matter. It only needed a few moments to take everything from me, everything inside of me.

In time, some shattered fragments of "me" returned, like metal shavings drawn to a toy magnet. I realized that I was not dead. I was still breathing. But I would never again think or feel the things that human beings are supposed to think or feel, simply by nature of being human.

Time passed, and I viewed my actions, my internal and external lives, as if observing from the grave. I was visible, but not present. And I could find no one, no other human who felt as I did.

I discovered a comfort in writing, literature, and the arts, which reveal the mind's hidden inner workings. I read voices and viewed images that on occasion reflected my inner world, but never completely.

I was neither depressed, nor anxious, nor happy, nor unhappy. I was not crazy because I knew that something was not right from the very moment that it became *not right*.

Things happen to people, I reasoned. Usually they happen to someone else. But this time it had happened to me, far too early in life. And it was something no one else understood. I would have opted for cancer, or war wounds, or polio if given a choice.

Instead, this thing had taken my soul but it had left me to idle here among the living, a vacuous robot with the task of still living an interminably long life before me. I wanted nothing more than to be an old, old man, with my life behind me.

Looking for Answers

For eleven years, a strange and terrifying mental state occupied my being, and I could not find one piece of information that described my condition or anything like it. Convinced that I was going insane, I eventually learned that I wasn't. But I suffered in ways that even now are near impossible to describe. At times this condition lifted enough for me to attempt to continue my life, as if I were just like anyone else. At other times it got worse, and I went to doctor after doctor looking for answers.

I visited more than a dozen doctors, several psychiatrists. Each prescribed a medication that knocked me out for a few days, and then, after weeks, brought me up to a functional level. A level wherein I resumed the lower-level suffering that allowed me to be a student, or take on a job. Happiness, well being, a functioning ego were not even secondary considerations. Maintaining the façade that convinced others I was normal, even intelligent or funny, was all that mattered.

Sometimes, my humanity returned through drinking. The everpresent viewing of my own life became a film noir, a black-and-white movie with dramatic outcomes, tears, and emotional overload, before the hammer of the hangover struck and killed the projectionist.

Decades of a lifetime passed. And after years of traveling the country, moving from job to job, relationship to relationship, apartment to apartment, in one remarkable meeting with one remarkably human and humane specialist, I learned that what I suffered from had a name.

I learned that the condition was not uncommon, but just the opposite—it was the third most common psychiatric symptom, after depression and anxiety. I learned that this strange unfathomable state of mind had been studied in Europe and in the U.S. for more than 100 years, and that there were dozens of clinical papers that had very clearly described every one of my symptoms. People suffered with it in silence for fear of being called crazy. Sometimes, they took their own lives as one final demonstration of control. I had been robbed of more than a decade of my life, wandering like a blind man only to discover that my eyes still functioned. They were merely covered by a blindfold created by the complacency of doctors who refused to acknowledge an illness outside of their typical retinue of diagnosis and treatment. This thing, this "filth" that had blinded me is called Depersonalization Disorder. The very name described what I had been searching for all along—my self, my personhood, which had somehow been deactivated.

This is the story of a condition endured by millions of people worldwide, most of whom have no idea that it has a name. [My] book is, to some degree, autobiographical. But who I am, where I come from, the specific path of my life hardly matters except for its resemblance to the lives of so many others. How deeply this filth determined the course of my life will always be a source of wonder for me. Through a time-honored medicine and undiminished "capacity for insight" I was able to live a life of my own, even as others were encountering depersonalization for the first time.

A Woman Recalls Living with Multiple Personalities

Karen Overhill, as told to Anne Underwood

In this interview from *Newsweek* magazine, a woman with dissociative identity disorder who had seventeen alternate personalities ("alters") describes what it was like before treatment enabled her to integrate them. Switching from one alter to another came over her like a wave, she says, and she felt as if she were about to faint. She lost time when she was unaware of what had happened to some alters, though she found things they had bought and books that they were reading. Some of them had their own friends that were strangers to her when she encountered them. She had some awareness of the child abuse she suffered at the time it was happening but felt no pain because it happened to the alters rather than to her. Later, during treatment, she recalled all their memories, which was confusing and exhausting.

Karen Overhill (a pseudonym) is the subject of a book by her doctor, Richard Baer, who describes her experiences and his treatment of her over many years. Anne Underwood is a reporter for *Newsweek*.

Multiple personality disorder is a perplexing phenomenon to outside observers, believed to be brought on by persistent childhood abuse. What is it like living with MPD? And how does a sufferer function, with so many alternate personalities—or "alters"—some of them adults and some children? *Newsweek*'s Anne Underwood spoke with Karen Overhill—a former sufferer and the subject of a new book, *Switching Time*, by Dr. Richard Baer.

Newsweek: When an alternate personality would emerge, your own consciousness receded. You called it "losing time," since you were unaware of what the alter said and did during that time. What does it feel like when an alter is taking over?

Karen Overhill: It feels like you're tuning out, about to faint. It would come like a wave over me. When I came back to myself I would be exhausted. I never knew where I'd been or what I'd done, so I would have to look for clues, like a bag in the car or leftovers from a restaurant. [One of the adult alters] would go for long drives at night. In the morning the gas tank would be empty, and there would be hundreds of miles on the odometer. I would wonder, 'Where did I go?' It was amazing, but I accepted it.

You had 17 alters. Before therapy, were you aware of their existence?

All I knew was that I was losing time. But there were signs. Clothes would come back from the cleaner's with Katherine's name on them. There were different books being read at the same time. There were things bought that I didn't remember purchasing. I only got to know the alters during therapy.

Some of the alters had their own friends. Did people call you by different names?

I would answer to anything, because I had no idea. I would just go with the flow. In a store, when I ran into someone I knew but didn't know, there would be a delayed reaction, like someone hit the pause button, until the alter who knew that person came out. I would remember walking up to that person. Then I would know nothing more until I got into the car. Once I got in the car and came back to myself, I'd think, 'Well, at least I got what I needed.'

Experts say that alternate personalities are formed to shield MPD sufferers from pain and memories of abuse. Did you have any awareness of the abuse you endured as a child?

I had some awareness of it at the time. I would see bruises and cuts. I had bits and pieces of memories, but you don't want to ask too many questions as a child for fear of it leading to more abuse. Later, during therapy, I asked questions of my mother and brothers in a roundabout way to try and confirm what had gone on. Sometimes I remembered horrible things, but I couldn't remember feeling pain, because the alters had taken it away.

You truly felt no pain?

The pain would be removed from me. Different alters would feel it. If I had a bad headache and I couldn't handle it, it would somehow just go away without medication. I wish I knew how to do it today. But this caused problems, too, because pain is protective. Once I stayed at work till the end of the day when I needed an appendectomy.

How is it possible that people around you as a child didn't notice that you were being abused? Why didn't teachers help you?

It wasn't like today, where you mention abuse and everyone comes running. In those days people whipped and beat their children. I went to Catholic school. If teachers saw welts, they thought it was discipline. And I thought I was bad and deserved punishment, so I didn't complain. No one would have believed me anyway, because Elise [the alter who was formed to go to school and behave like a normal child] didn't act abused. My father and grandfather had said that if I ever told anyone,

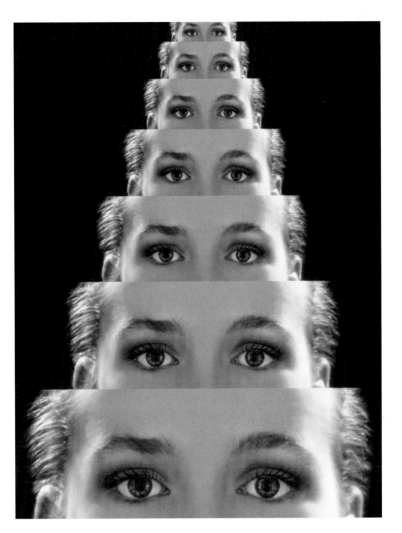

Karen Overhill, who claims to have had seventeen different personalities, describes her experience of switching from one to another as a feeling of growing faint, which came over her like a wave. (© **Mehau Kulyk/ Photo Researchers, Inc.**)

they would kill me. So I put makeup over the wounds or wore long pants if I had bruises. I was careful to cover up signs. When I got to high school it became harder for my grandfather and father because I went to a much larger school that was farther away. They made me come home right away after school so that I wouldn't talk. I didn't have girlfriends, because I wasn't allowed to go to their homes. When I was invited to slumber parties, my parents would say, "She's too sick. She can't come." Eventually my classmates stopped asking.

What was it like during therapy, as each alter gave up its independent existence and was reintegrated into you—Karen?

Each time I went through an integration, it was exhausting. I was receiving all their memories. And there were physical issues, too. One alter would want to do things left-handed and the others right-handed. Lots of the alters had different walks. After integrating one of the child alters, I didn't know how to drive. That wasn't a good day. I sideswiped a car coming out of the parking lot.

It gives a whole new meaning to the phrase "identity crisis."

With each integration I would become a different person. If someone asked me what kind of music I liked, I didn't know. I would have to figure it out, because the alters liked different music. I'm still trying to figure out who I am. It took a year or so before I began feeling all the alters were me.

Was it hard learning to live as a whole person again?

At first, when I couldn't lose time, I would get stressed and overwhelmed. There was no escape. I kept saying to Dr. Baer, "I should have kept one alter as a spare, to lose time to." But really, being reintegrated felt like waking up after being in a coma. My life started over in 1998 [when the process was complete].

After reintegration, you found that Katherine had a lot of friends you didn't know. How did you deal with them?

I didn't like a lot of Katherine's friends, and they didn't like me. They were looking for the same person they'd known before. It was kind of sad, because I couldn't be that person for them. I tried to respect Katherine's choices and stay in the relationships, but I didn't really know these people. I faked illnesses a lot to get out of meeting with them. Eventually some faded away. I was grateful for that. "Karen 2" had friendships too, but not enduring ones. Ann's friends were more the church types. I've stayed friends with a few of them, because they were good people. But for the most part I had to make all new friends.

How can you survive the kind of treatment you endured without tremendous anger?

I can't harp on that. I have to move on.

What are your plans now?

I'm still trying to figure that out. When you're suicidal, as I was for so long, you don't make long-range plans. But I like working with people. The funny thing is, most people my age have settled down and are looking forward to retirement. I'm just thinking about registering for college. But the most important thing for me is just knowing that I'm alive and can look forward to the future.

A Woman Explains How False Memories Led Her to Believe She Had Multiple Personality Disorder

Lauri

Lauri is one of many women who have retracted accusations against their parents after learning that their alleged "memories" of being sexually abused were false. She tells here how she wanted to please her therapist and how he convinced her that she would need many years of expensive treatment to recover her repressed memories. She explains how he implanted false memories—which he considered true—during hypnosis intended to help her recall childhood experiences. Finally, when she had "remembered" taking part in satanic rituals, she was horrified and became suicidal. Though she showed all the symptoms of multiple personality disorder (MPD), she had learned them by behaving as the therapist expected until eventually they took over her mind.

SOURCE: Lauri, "Retractors Speak: The Therapy—Learned MPD," False Memory Syndrome Foundation, January 1994. © 2008 by False Memory Syndrome Foundation. All rights reserved. Reproduced by permission.

I was not the only MPD [multiple personality disorder] patient. My therapist had a group of five women participating in this dysfunctional, cult-like treatment. Our therapist was using mind games to control us and convince us he was the only person who could help us. In "private", he would drop comments about the other MPD "girls." As patients, we became very competitive and jealous of each other.

I was especially jealous of one woman who was very pretty. He had made sexual advances toward one of her sexiest alters, and I was convinced he was infatuated with her. He would play his guitar and sing for her, but never me. He compared the two of us and said we were very much alike. He often confused our names which made me feel hurt. I wanted him to like me in the way he liked her.

I clearly understood the sickest patient received the most attention. So, I devised behavior that would get his attention: act like a five-year-old, come intoxicated to my session, threaten him with a knife, or even attempt suicide. Everyone of us in the support group were in some way in love with our psychologist.

I wanted to be the best. I became a model MPD patient and exhibited all the right traits. I learned MPD and let it in, but soon it took control of my mind and body.

The doctor decided I needed five to seven years of therapy. He explained to me and my husband, "Because Lauri now has MPD behavior, it follows that she had MPD. Thus, some terrible abuse in her childhood must have caused it. So terrible that she's repressed those memories deep in her mind. With my help, the alters will reveal the abuse, then she'll remember her own experiences. Finally, she will work through those old feelings and get better."

This is about the time he raised his rates to $120 per hour.

The Creation of False Memories

We bought it, and I worked hard to recall repressed memories. Of course, there were no real memories, but the mind is an amazing thing. Let me explain, in lay terms, how repressed memories were created on one occasion. The therapist called up Beth, a 5-year-old alter, and hypnotized her. He suggested sexual abuse had occurred at the hands of her Daddy. He explained she needed to see a "big movie screen" in her mind and tell him what she saw. Then, he asked leading questions about touching, etc. Beth performed just as the therapist predicted she would. Beth and I were rewarded with much attention and sympathy.

In reality, I didn't have those memories, but the doctor considered them true and wanted more. For months, I allowed other alters to write anything they could remember. The memories grew worse and worse and I became horrified. I thought it was all true, and I felt worthless and betrayed.

I recalled various fragments of movies, books, talk shows, and nightly news, and soon I had plenty of child abuse memories. But, it didn't stop there. Eventually, I said I had taken part in Satanic Rituals, been buried alive, drank blood, and helped to kill a baby. With every new memory, my therapist was intrigued and building a case to prove he was right about me all along. I was rewarded with his attention to me and was his "best" patient. But, I started to have feelings of death and became suicidal.

I truly exhibited all the MPD symptoms even though I had learned them. Control of my mind, emotions, and will was given to the personalities the therapist had empowered.

GLOSSARY

alter	One of the personality states of a person with dissociative identity disorder.
comorbid	Refers to two or more medical or psychiatric conditions affecting a person at the same time.
complex PTSD	A form of post-traumatic stress disorder that includes dissociative symptoms.
confabulation	Fabrication of answers to questions about past situations or events by a person who is unable to recall them.
core or core self	In reference to dissociative disorders, the original personality state of a person with dissociative identity disorder.
covert switch	An unconscious and unperceivable switch between the personalities or states of a person with dissociative identity disorder.
depersonalization	A dissociative disorder involving persistent or recurrent experiences of feeling detached from one's mental processes and/or body.
derealization	A feeling of estrangement or detachment from one's environment, or a sense that the external world is strange or unreal.
Diagnostic and Statistical Manual of Mental Disorders	The official diagnostic manual of the American Psychiatric Association, usually referred to as DSM, followed by roman numerals denoting the current edition.
dissociation	A state of consciousness in which a person feels detached from what is happening, and/or from his or her thoughts, memories, or identity. Mild, brief dissociation is normal. Dissociation can also be a normal temporary response to trauma. If it continues or recurs frequently, it is considered a disorder.

dissociative amnesia	One or more episodes of inability to recall important personal information, usually of a traumatic or stressful nature, that is too extensive to be explained by ordinary forgetfulness.
dissociative disorder not otherwise specified (DDNOS)	A diagnostic category for individuals who have dissociative symptoms but do not meet the minimum criteria for any of the specific dissociative disorders.
Dissociative Experiences Scale (DES)	A self-reported questionnaire asking the respondent to indicate the frequency with which certain dissociative or depersonalization experiences occur.
dissociative fugue	A dissociative disorder or experience involving sudden, un-expected travel from home or work with the inability to recall some or all of one's past, sometimes including assumption of a new identity.
dissociative identity disorder (DID)	A dissociative disorder involving the presence of two or more distinct identities or personality states, at least two of which re-currently take control of the person's behavior. This condition was formerly called multiple personality disorder (MPD).
false memory	A memory of something that never actually happened that seems real to a person. False memories can be inadvertently implanted by techniques intended to recall true memories.
false memory syndrome (FMS)	A term defined by the False Memory Syndrome Foundation (FMSF) as "a condition in which the person's personality and interpersonal relationships are oriented around a memory that is objectively false but strongly believed in to the detriment of the welfare of the person and others involved in the memory." This is not a diagnostic category but merely a description of what some people experience.
front	The mental position or state of mind in which a person with dissociative identity disorder is controlling the body, interacting with the world at large.
fugue	*See* dissociative fugue.

hypnosis	An altered state of consciousness different from normal alertness, often induced by therapists to facilitate recovery of a person's memories and in treatment of DID to facilitate communication between personality states, as well as for purposes unrelated to dissociative disorders.
iatrogenic	Refers to an illness caused or aggravated by medical treatment or psychotherapy. Some psychiatrists believe that DID is an iatrogenic illness, produced by a client to meet the expectations of a therapist.
integration	The ongoing process of bringing together all dissociated aspects of a person, whether they are thoughts, feelings, or behaviors or are organized as personality states or fragments. Integration was formerly the goal in treating DID, but currently this is controversial.
losing time	In reference to dissociative disorders, having no recollection of one's activities during a given time.
multiple, multiplicity	Refers to two or more personalities in the same body—either the collective itself, the entire group within the shared body, or the main front or person first met.
multiple personality disorder (MPD)	The former name for dissociative identity disorder.
personality state	An aspect of a person with dissociative identity disorder that has a consistent and ongoing set of response patterns to given stimuli, a significant confluent history, a range of emotions available (anger, sadness, joy, and so on), and a range of intensity for each emotion.
post-traumatic stress disorder (PTSD)	An anxiety disorder arising from an individual's response to a traumatic event that involved actual or threatened death or serious injury, or a threat to the physical integrity of self or others, where the person's response involved intense fear, helplessness, or horror.
psychogenic or psychological amnesia	The former name for dissociative amnesia.

recovered memory   A repressed memory that surfaces long after the event, either spontaneously or during therapy. Many experts believe that most if not all recovered memories are false memories inadvertently created by therapists.

recovered-memory therapy (RMT)   Any of various unproven psychotherapeutic techniques used with the aim of recovering repressed memories of past abuse. Such methods, though never officially approved, were commonly used in the 1980s; they are rarely used today by responsible therapists.

repressed memory   A memory of something that actually happened of which a person is not aware. Some experts believe repressed memories are rare or nonexistent, while others believe they are common.

repression   An unconscious defense mechanism that occurs when unacceptable ideas, images, or fantasies are kept out of awareness.

screen memory   A partially true memory that an individual subconsciously creates because the actual memory is intolerable.

splitting   In reference to DID, the act of creating new personalities from a core self.

state-dependent memory   Information and events remembered only when in the same emotional or physiological state in which it was learned or in which the events happened or were dreamed.

switching   In a person with dissociative identity disorder, the process of changing from one already existing personality state to another.

trauma   A medical term for any sudden injury or damage to an organism. Psychological trauma is an event that is outside the range of usual human experience and that is so seriously distressing as to cause lasting emotional harm.

CHRONOLOGY

19th Century   The concept of dissociation is recognized and investigated, especially by hypnotists, and a few cases of multiple personalities are noted by medical science.

1886   Robert Louis Stevenson's novel *The Strange Case of Dr Jekyll and Mr Hyde* is published. This is the first popular presentation of a person with a "split personality"; i.e., two or more different personality states.

1890s   French psychologist Pierre Janet coins the term *dissociation* and develops influential theories about it, including the idea that it is a result of psychological trauma.

1956   *The Three Faces of Eve*, a fictionalized story of a woman with three personalities presented as a documentary, is published, bringing multiple personality disorder (MPD) to the attention of the public. The next year it is made into a hit movie, attracting further notice.

1968   MPD is defined in the American Psychiatric Association's *Diagnostic and Statistical Manual of Mental Disorders* as a hysterical neurosis.

1973   The book *Sybil*, about a woman believed to have sixteen personalities, is published, describing her experience in therapy.

1976   The broadcast of *Sybil* as a TV miniseries has a major impact on the public's perception of MPD.

1979   A study finds that until this time there have been only two hundred cases of MPD in all recorded medical history. During the 1980s the number of cases increases to twenty thousand. There are a number of conflicting explanations for this rise.

1980   A new edition of the American Psychiatric Association's manual, DSM-III, defines dissociation as "a disturbance or alteration in the normally integrative functions of identity, memory or consciousness" and lists MPD as one of four dissociative disorders.

1988   *The Courage to Heal* is published, becoming a best seller and leading large numbers of women to "recover" memories of childhood sexual abuse that they are convinced they had repressed. This results in many bitter court battles and sometimes in the imprisonment of innocent parents.

1990s   Evidence is produced that apparent memories supposedly lost through dissociative amnesia are sometimes false and may have been inadvertently created during therapy. In the backlash against the recovered-memory therapy movement, which had caused serious harm to many people, some women successfully sue their therapists for implanting false memories. The issue is hotly debated throughout the decade and as of 2012 is still controversial.

1994   The American Psychiatric Association renames MPD dissociative identity disorder (DID) in its revised diagnostic manual, DSM-IV.

2000s   Both recovered memories and DID become increasingly controversial, with the pendulum swinging away from belief that they are genuine conditions, and toward the belief that they are unintentionally created by the assumptions of therapists.

ORGANIZATIONS TO CONTACT

The editors have compiled the following list of organizations concerned with the issues debated in this book. The descriptions are derived from materials provided by the organizations. All have publications or information available for interested readers. The list was compiled on the date of publication of the present volume; the information provided here may change. Be aware that many organizations take several weeks or longer to respond to inquiries, so allow as much time as possible.

DSM-5 Development
American Psychiatric Association
1000 Wilson Blvd., Ste. 1825, Arlington, VA 22209-3901
(703) 907-7300
e-mail: apa@psych.org
website: www.dsm5.org

This site contains information about the pending revision of the *Diagnostic and Statistical Manual of Mental Disorders* (DSM), which is the standard classification of mental disorders used by mental health professionals in the United States for diagnosis. It includes the proposed revised categories of dissociative disorders and the criteria by which they will be diagnosed.

False Memory Syndrome Foundation (FMSF)
1955 Locust St., Philadelphia, PA 19103-5766
(215) 940-1040
fax: (215) 940-1042
e-mail: mail@fmsf online.org
website: www.fmsf online.org

The FMSF is a nonprofit organization that investigates the reasons behind false memory syndrome, works toward ways to prevent it, and seeks to aid those who were affected by it and to bring their families into reconciliation. It was founded by parents who had been falsely accused of having abused their now-adult children when the children were young on the basis of memories that had supposedly been repressed. It contains information about false memories and stories of people who have become aware that the memories they allegedly recovered during therapy were false and who have retracted their accusations against their parents.

International Society for the Study of Trauma and Dissociation (ISST-D)
8400 Westpark Dr., 2nd Fl., McLean, VA 22102
(703) 610-9037
fax: (703) 610-0234
e-mail: info@isst-d.org
website: www.isst-d.org

ISST-D is a nonprofit professional association that seeks to advance clinical, scientific, and societal understanding about the prevalence and consequences of chronic trauma and dissociation. Its website contains information about dissociative disorders and other consequences of trauma, plus resources recommended for students.

Psych Central
55 Pleasant St., Ste. 207, Newburyport, MA 01950
(978) 225-0711
e-mail: talkback@psych central.com
website: http://psych central.com

Psych Central is the Internet's largest and oldest independent mental health and psychology network. Since 1995 it has been run by mental health professionals offering reliable information and over 160 support groups to consumers and has been noted in major national magazines. It contains descriptions of all psychological disorders, including dissociative disorders; information about research studies; and links to support groups and other resources.

Recovered Memory Project
Taub Center for Public Policy & American Institutions 67 George St., Box 1977, Brown University, Providence, RI 02912
website: http://blogs .brown.edu/recovered memory

The Recovered Memory Project collects and disseminates information relevant to the debate over the question of whether traumatic events can be forgotten and then remembered later in life. It opposes the concept of false memory. Its website contains an archive describing legal and clinical cases involving recovered memories plus resource material about dissociative amnesia.

Sidran Institute
PO Box 436,
Brooklandville, MD
21022-0436
(410) 825-8888 • fax:
(410) 560-0134
e-mail: info@sidran.org
website: www.sidran.org

The Sidran Institute is a nonprofit organization that helps people understand, manage, and treat trauma and dissociation. It develops educational programs and resources for treatment and self-help, and puts out publications. Its website has many articles on all aspects of trauma plus links to other resources and lists of recommended books.

Valor Institute
2100 Riverside Pkwy.,
Ste. 119, #503,
Lawrenceville, GA
30043
website: www.valor
institute.org

The Valor Institute is a nonprofit organization dedicated to serving clients who are healing from dissociative disorders of a traumatic origin. Its ValorNet communities specifically serve those who are working to overcome dissociative identity disorder and dissociative disorder not otherwise specified. Its website contains information about dissociative disorders and about working with a therapist, plus a directory of therapists.

FOR FURTHER READING

Books

Suzette Boon, Kathy Steele, and Onno van der Hart. *Coping with Trauma-Related Dissociation.* New York: Norton, 2011.

James A. Chu, *Rebuilding Shattered Lives: Treating Complex PTSD and Dissociative Disorders.* New York: Wiley, 2011.

Susan A. Clancy, *The Trauma Myth: The Truth About the Sexual Abuse of Children—and Its Aftermath.* New York: Basic Books, 2011.

Paul F. Dell and John A. O'Neill, *Dissociation and the Dissociative Disorders: DSM-V and Beyond.* New York: Routledge, 2009.

Onno van der Hart, Ellert R.S. Nijenhuis, and Kathy Steele, *The Haunted Self: Structural Dissociation and the Treatment of Chronic Traumatization.* New York: Norton, 2006.

Elizabeth Howell, *The Dissociative Mind.* New York: Routledge, 2005.

———, *Understanding and Treating Dissociative Identity Disorder: A Relational Approach.* New York: Routledge, 2011.

Marlene E. Hunter, *Understanding Dissociative Disorders: A Guide for Family Physicians and Health Care Professionals.* New York: Crown, 2009.

Jane Hyman, *I Am More than One.* New York: McGraw-Hill, 2006.

Meredith Maran, *My Lie: A True Story of False Memory.* San Francisco: Jossey-Bass, 2010.

Paul R. McHugh, *Try to Remember: Psychiatry's Clash Over Meaning, Memory, and Mind.* New York: Dana, 2008.

Debbie Nathan, *Sybil Exposed: The Extraordinary Story Behind the Famous Multiple Personality Case.* New York: Free Press, 2011.

Fugen Neziroglu, Katharine Donnelly, and Daphne Simeon, *Overcoming Depersonalization Disorder: A Mindfulness and Acceptance Guide to Conquering Feelings of Numbness and Unreality*. Oakland, CA: New Harbinger, 2010.

Karl Sabbagh, *Remembering Our Childhood: How Memory Betrays Us*. New York: Oxford University Press, 2009.

Adad Sachs, *Forensic Aspects of Dissociative Identity Disorder*. London: Karnac, 2008.

Daphne Simeon and Jeffrey Abugel, *Feeling Unreal: Depersonalization Disorder and the Loss of the Self*. New York: Oxford University Press, 2008.

Valerie Sinason, *Understanding and Treating Dissociative Identity Disorder*. New York: Routledge, 2011.

Olga Trujillo, *The Sum of My Parts: A Survivor's Story of Dissociative Identity Disorder*. Oakland, CA: New Harbinger, 2011.

Herschel Walker, *Breaking Free: My Life with Dissociative Identity Disorder*. New York: Touchstone, 2009.

Periodicals and Internet Sources

Dominique Bourget and Laurie Whitehurst, "Amnesia and Crime," *Journal of the American Academy of Psychiatry and the Law*, December 2007. www.jaapl.org/content/35/4/469.full.

Jane E. Brody, "When a Brain Forgets Where Memory Is," *New York Times*, April 17, 2007.

Theodore Dalrymple, "Destructive Delusions," *Wall Street Journal*, November 20, 2008. http://online.wsj.com/article/SB12271 4489697843157.html.

Anda Davies, "A Brief Introduction to Dissociation," Australian Institute of Professional Counselors, May 25, 2010. www.aipc .net.au/articles/?p=215.

Paul F. Dell, *Understanding Dissociation* (blog). http://under standingdissociation.com.

Mirian Falco, "Herschel Walker Reveals Many Sides of Himself," CNN.com, April 15, 2008. http://edition.cnn.com/2008 /HEALTH/conditions/04/15/herschel.walker.did/.

Helen M. Farrell, "Dissociative Identity Disorder: No Excuse for Criminal Activity," *Current Psychiatry*, June 2011. www.current psychiatry.com/pdf/1006/1006CP_Article3.pdf.

Numan Gharaibeh, "Dissociative Identity Disorder: Time to Remove It from DSM-V?," *Current Psychiatry*, September 2009. www.ptsdforum.org/c/gallery/-pdf/l-39.pdf.

Holly Gray, "*The Hunger Games*, Dissociative Identity Disorder, and PTSD," *Dissociative Living* (blog), April 18, 2011. www .healthyplace.com/blogs/dissociativeliving/2011/04/the-hunger -games-dissociative-identity-disorder-and-ptsd/.

John H. Kihlstrom, "Trauma and Memory Revisited," 6th Tsukuba International Conference on Memory, March 15, 2005. http://socrates.berkeley.edu/~kihlstrm/Tsukuba05.htm.

Kelly Lambert and Scott O. Lilienfeld, "Brain Stains," *Scientific American*, October 2007.

Julia Layton, "5 Myths About Dissociative Identity Disorder," *Discovery*, n.d., http://health.discovery.com/tv/psych-week /articles/myths-about-dissociative-identiry-disorder.html.

Elizabeth F. Loftus, "Make-Believe Memories," *American Psychologist*, November 2003. http://faculty.washington.edu/eloftus /Articles/AmerPsychAward+ArticlePDF03%20%282%29.pdf.

Elizabeth F. Loftus, Maryanne Garry, and Harlene Hayne, "Repressed and Recovered Memory," in *Beyond Common Sense: Psychological Science In The Courtroom*, edited by Eugene Borgida and Susan T. Fiske. *UC Irvine School of Law Research Paper No. 2009-13*, 2007. http://ssrn.com/abstract=1375023.

Rebecca Flint Marx and Vytenis Didziulis, "A Life Interrupted," *New York Times*, February 27, 2009.

Stephen Mason, "Recovery Memory Syndrome: A Modern Witch Hunt," *Psychology Today* (blogs), January 6, 2010. www .psychologytoday.com/blog/look-it-way/201001 /recovered -memory-syndrome.

Jean Mercer, "The Paul Shanley Case and Repressed Memory Recovery: Not Such Thin Partitions," *Psychology Today* (blogs), January 17, 2010. www.psychologytoday.com/blog/child-myths /201001/the-paul-shanley-case-and-repressed-memory-recovery -not-such-thin-partitions.

Veronica Pamoukaghlian, "Behind the Masks: The Mysteries of Dissociative Identity Disorder," *Brain Blogger,* August 28, 2011. http://brainblogger.com/2011/08/28/behind-the-masks-the -mysteries-of-dissociative-identity-disorder/.

Ashley Pettus, "Repressed Memory," *Harvard Magazine,* January– February 2008. http://harvardmagazine.com/2008/01/repressed -memory.html.

Katherine Ramsland and Rachel Kuter, "Multiple Personalities: Crime and Defense," *TruTV Crime Library,* n.d. www.trutv.com /library/crime/criminal_mind/psychology/multiples/.

B.A. Robinson, "Multiple Personality Disorder (MPD) & Dis- sociative Identity Disorder (DID): All Sides to the Debate," On- tario Consultants on Religious Tolerance, September 13, 2009. www.religioustolerance.org/mpd_did.htm#menu.

Henry L. Roediger III and Elizabeth J. Marsh, "False Memory," *Scholarpedia,* 2009. www.scholarpedia.org/article/False_memory.

David Spiegel, "Coming Apart: Trauma and the Fragmentation of the Self," Dana Foundation, January 31, 2008. www.dana.org /news/cerebrum/detail.aspx?id=11122.

———, "Dissociation in the DSM5," *Journal of Trauma & Dis- sociation,* July 2010. www.tandfonline.com/doi/full/10.1080 /15299731003780788.

David Van Nuys, "Wise Counsel Interview Transcript: An In- terview with John Kihlstrom, Ph.D. on Hypnosis, Dissociation and Trauma," Emergency Health Network, n.d. http://info .epmhmr.org/poc/view_doc.php?type=doc&id=27004.

Katie Zezima and Benedict Carey, "Ex-priest Challenges Abuse Conviction on Repressed Memories," *New York Times,* Septem- ber 10, 2009.

Websites   Astraea's Web (www.astraeasweb.net/plural). Astraea's Web contains many articles, links, and other resource information about dissociative identity disorder, taking the position that having multiple personalities is not an illness if a person can function well with them.

INDEX